pathfinder® guide

Lake District

WALKS

Compiled by
Brian Conduit

JARROLD

Acknowledgements
I would like to thank Mr R. Cartwright (Head of National Park
Management) and his staff, as well as Mr P.J. Battrick (Assistant
Regional Information Officer for the National Trust) for looking
at the manuscript and giving me much useful advice. The
publishers also wish to thank Mr David Woodhead, Ravenglass,
of the Ramblers' Association for checking information, and
the Lake District National Park Authority: Ms Sue Arnott
(Rights of Way Officer) and Mr Scott Henderson (Area Ranger)
helped to update information, and Ms Judith Quigley (Interpretation Projects Officer) and Mr Guy Huxtable (Commerical
Buyer) provided the text on page 13.

Text: Brian Conduit
Photography: Brian Conduit and Jarrold Publishing
Editor: Geoffrey Sutton
Designers: Brian Skinner, Doug Whitworth

Series Consultant: Brian Conduit

Jarrold Publishing   ISBN 0-7117-0463-5

While every care has been taken to ensure the accuracy of the
route directions, the publishers cannot accept responsibility
for errors or omissions, or for changes in details given. The
countryside is not static: hedges and fences can be removed,
field boundaries can be altered, footpaths can be rerouted and
changes in ownership can result in the closure or diversion
of some concessionary paths. Also, paths that are easy and
pleasant for walking in fine conditions may become slippery,
muddy and difficult in wet weather, while stepping-stones
across rivers and streams may become impassable.

If you find an inaccuracy in either the text or maps, please
write to Jarrold Publishing at the address below.

First published 1989
by Jarrold Publishing and Ordnance Survey
Revised and reprinted 1990, 1991, 1992, 1996, 1998, 1999,
2001.

Printed in Belgium
by Proost NV, Turnhout. 8/01

Jarrold Publishing
Pathfinder Guides, Whitefriars, Norwich NR3 1TR
E-mail: pathfinder@jarrold.com

Front cover: The head of Wast Water
Previous page: Castlerigg Stone Circle

Contents

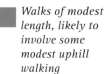 Short, easy walks

Walks of modest length, likely to involve some modest uphill walking

More challenging walks which may be longer and/or over more rugged terrain, often with some stiff climbs

Keymap

Camerton · Bridgefoot · Brigham · Embleton · A66

Great Clifton · Greysouthen

WORKINGTON

A66 · Eaglesfield · 310 · 332 · 1225

A596 · A595 · Deanscales · Lorton · B5292 · Lord's S...

Moss Bay · Dean · Pardshaw · 1364 · Grisedale S... · 2599

Harrington · Branthwaite · Mockerkin · Grasmoor · 2791

Distington · Ullock · 1 · Loweswater · 2791

Lowca · Gilgarran · Asby · Lamplugh · Loweswater Fell · Crummock Water · Buttermere

WHITEHAVEN · Pica · 565 · 811 · Loweswater · 1878 · 1676

Moresby · Arlecdon · 691 · Murton Fell · Great Borne · Buttermere

Moresby Parks · Frizington · 13 · 2020 · 19 · 21

Saltom Bay · Ennerdale Bridge · High Stile · 2644

CLEATOR MOOR · Grike · Ennerdale Water · 2241

Sandwith · 462 · Cleator · Lank Rigg · Ennerdale Fell · Pillar · 2927

Rottington · Bigrigg · 2207 · Scoat Fell · 2760 · Black Sail

St Bees · EGREMONT · Caw Fell · Haycock · 2629 · Kirk Fell

469 · 695 · Seatallan · 2270 · COPELAND FOREST · Wasdale Head · Lingm...

Nethertown · Haile · 950 · R. Calder · 1056 · R. Bleng · Nether Wasdale · 12 · West Water · Burnmoor Tarn · 1983 · 1105

Beckermet · Calder Bridge · R. Irt · Santon Bridge · Boot · ROM...

Braystones · Works · Gosforth · Outward Bound Mountain School · Beckfoot · 3

Sellafield Sta · B5344 · A595 · 221 · Eskdale Green · Stanley Force · Birker Force

Seascale · Holmrook · River Mite · 758 · River Esk · Devoke Water

Drigg · 98 · Ravenglass · Muncaster Castle · Woodend · Ulpha Fell

Kokoarrah · 15 · Waberthwaite · Whitfell · 1881 · Ulpha

Tarn Bay · Corney · Prior Park · Stoneside Hill · Duddon Bridge

Selker Bay · Hycemoor · Bootle Sta · Bootle · Bootle Fell

Annaside · Black Combe · 1970 · 12 · Hallthwaite

Whitbeck · A595 · The Green · Gr... Sta

Whicham · The Hill · A5093

Silecroft · MILLOM

Kirksanton · Askam · Furnes...

Haverigg · Duddon

At-a-glance...

Walk	Page	Start	Nat. Grid Reference	Distance	Time	Highest Point
Aira Force and Dockray	16	Aira Force	NY 400200	3½ miles (5.6km)	1½ hrs	820ft (250m)
Ashness Bridge, Watendlath and Bowder Stone	70	Kettlewell	NY 267194	8½ miles (13.7km)	5 hrs	1083ft (330m)
Back of Bowness	24	Bowness-on-Windermere	SD 403969	4 miles (6.4km)	2½ hrs	590ft (180m)
Birks Bridge, Hardknott and Harter Fell	76	Birks Bridge	SD 235995	7 miles (11.3km)	4 hrs	2140ft (653m)
Borrowdale	34	Seatoller	NY 245137	7 miles (11.3km)	3½ hrs	787ft (240m)
Buttermere and Hay Stacks	67	Buttermere	NY 174169	7½ miles (12.1km)	5 hrs	1900ft (579m)
Cartmel and Hampsfield Fell	37	Cartmel	SD 378787	7 miles (11.3km)	4 hrs	673ft (205m)
Cat Bells and Derwent Water	56	Hawes End	NY 247212	4½ miles (7.2km)	2½ hrs	1481ft (451m)
Coniston Old Man and Coniston Water	87	Coniston	SD 303975	9 miles (14.5km)	5½ hrs	2635ft (803m)
Crummock Water, Mosedale and Rannerdale	61	Buttermere	NY 174169	9½ miles (15.3km)	5 hrs	919ft (280m)
Dodd Wood and Bassenthwaite	20	Dodd Wood	NY 234281	3 miles (4.8 km)	1½ hrs	374ft (114m)
Elterwater and Skelwith Bridge	26	Elterwater	NY 327047	6 miles (9.7km)	3 hrs	525ft (160m)
Ennerdale Water	43	Ennerdale Water	NY 094161	8 miles (12.9km)	4 hrs	394ft (120m)
Friar's Crag and Castlerigg Stone Circle	46	Keswick	NY 264229	7 miles (11.3km)	3½ hrs	722ft (220m)
Grasmere and Rydal Water	31	Grasmere	NY 336074	5½ miles (8.9km)	3 hrs	459ft (140m)
Great and Little Langdale	52	New Dungeon Ghyll	NY 295064	8 miles (12.9km)	4 hrs	590ft (180m)
Great Gable	82	Seathwaite	NY 235122	6 miles (9.7km)	5 hrs	2949ft (899m)
Haweswater, High Street and Harter Fell	73	Haweswater	NY 469107	7 miles (11.3km)	4½ hrs	2719ft (828m)
Hawkshead and Tarn Hows	28	Hawkshead	SD 353980	6 miles (9.7km)	3 hrs	755ft (230m)
Helvellyn	84	Glenridding	NY 386169	8½ miles (13.7km)	6 hrs	3118ft (949m)
Loweswater	14	Loweswater	NY 118224	4 miles (6.4km)	2 hrs	656ft (200m)
Place Fell and Ullswater	79	Patterdale	NY 394160	8½ miles (13.7km)	5 hrs	2154ft (657m)
Ravenglass and Muncaster	49	Ravenglass	SD 084963	7 miles (11.3km)	4 hrs	295ft (90m)
Sawrey and Claife Heights	58	Far Sawrey	SD 388954	6½ miles (10.5km)	3½ hrs	886ft (270m)
Stanley Force and Eskdale	18	Dalegarth	NY 173006	4½ miles (7.2km)	2½ hrs	541ft (165m)
Thirlmere and Great How	22	Thirlmere	NY 315169	4 miles (6.4km)	2½ hrs	984ft (300m)
Wansfell and Troutbeck	64	Ambleside	NY 376046	6½ miles (10.5km)	4 hrs	1588ft (484m)
Wast Water and Irton Fell	40	Wast Water	NY 148049	6 miles (9.7km)	4 hrs	1280ft (390m)

Comments

A series of waterfalls, combined with superb views over Ullswater, creates a spectacular but at the same time easy walk.

An outstanding walk that takes in a number of spectacular viewpoints over Derwent Water and Borrowdale, an idyllic hamlet, and finishes with a stroll beside the lake.

From the higher points on this walk there are some outstanding views across Windermere.

Magnificent views over the Duddon valley and down Eskdale, especially from Hardknott Roman fort, can be enjoyed on this walk but be prepared for some steep and rough climbing.

Fine woodland and riverside walking, with views over mountains and lakes, enables you to judge for yourself if Borrowdale is, as often claimed, the loveliest valley in England.

A relaxing circuit of Buttermere can be combined with a steep and quite tiring climb to the summit of Hay Stacks to create a most memorable, satisfying and dramatic walk.

A walk in gentler country on the southern edge of the Lake District, but the views are still spectacular and there is a medieval priory to visit.

The short, sharp climb to Cat Bells rewards you with glorious views across Derwent Water. The last part of the walk is along the lakeshore.

The lengthy and quite steep ascent of the Old Man of Coniston is followed by a gradual descent and a relaxing finale by the lakeshore.

Dramatic views over both Crummock Water and Buttermere are seen on this lengthy but not particularly strenuous circuit of the former.

A climb through conifer woods, with views over Bassenthwaite Lake, is followed by a visit to a small church on the shores of the lake.

Woodlands and waterfalls dominate this walk, and towards the end comes one of the classic views of Lakeland, across Elter Water to the Langdale Pikes.

A lengthy but easy circuit of Ennerdale Water, the most remote of the lakes, with superb and ever-changing views all the way.

A prehistoric stone circle is the main focal point of this walk which gives magnificent views over Keswick, Derwent Water and Bassenthwaite.

Wordsworth is the main theme of this circuit of the small lakes of Grasmere and Rydal Water. The route passes two of his homes and his grave in the churchyard at Grasmere.

A spectacular walk that links the twin valleys of Great and Little Langdale and enables you to enjoy the exquisite views over Blea Tarn to the Langdale Pikes.

The wild and majestic scenery around Great Gable makes it deservedly one of the best-loved peaks in the Lake District.

A steep climb to the summit of High Street is followed by a superb ridge walk that gives outstanding views down the length of Haweswater.

Superb views can be enjoyed on this route that links the attractive village of Hawkshead with the rugged beauty of Tarn Hows.

The traverses of Striding Edge and the companion Swirral Edge below the summit of Helvellyn are definitely not for the inexperienced or faint-hearted.

This short and easy circuit of the lake passes through beautiful woodland along its western shores.

There are ever-changing views of Ullswater, both on the high-level outward route over Place Fell and on the return along an outstandingly beautiful path above the shores of the lake.

There is plenty of variety on this walk that includes seashore, woodland and fell, and passes the remains of a Roman fort and a castle.

From the thickly wooded Claife Heights there are a series of fine views across Windermere, but expect some rocky and muddy paths in places.

There is plenty of variety on this short and highly attractive walk in Eskdale.

An initial walk through woodland beside Thirlmere leads to the viewpoint of Great How. The return is along the fellside with fine views across the lake.

Both on the outward route over the summit of Wansfell and the lower-level return route, there are magnificent views down the length of Windermere.

Enjoy the air of mystery and lonely grandeur of Wast Water. The steep climb to Irton Fell is followed by a descent that gives magnificent views looking towards the head of Wasdale.

At-a-glance...

Introduction to the Lake District

If anyone can be said to have 'put the Lake District on the map', it must be the region's most famous son. The poetry of William Wordsworth, much of which describes and was inspired by the grandeur of the Lakes, encouraged some of the most eminent people of the day to venture into the area. This trickle of early tourists later developed into a stream, preparing the way for a mass invasion of tourists, which has now assumed torrential proportions.

Before the advent of tourism, isolation from the mainstream of national life had been the chief characteristic of the Lake District's history. The reason for this is obvious, and stems from its geographical location – tucked away in the far north-west corner of England, jutting out into the Irish Sea and almost cut off from the rest of the country by the long and wide inlets of Morecambe Bay on the south and the Solway Firth on the north, as well as by its own mountain barriers. To the west these mountains drop down to the Cumbrian coast and to the east (the landward side), the vales of Lune and Eden form a natural frontier.

Friendly and Welcoming Grandeur

This delectable landscape of lakes and mountains, valleys and waterfalls has captivated and enchanted millions of visitors but, at the same time, its unique scenic beauty is somewhat difficult to analyse. For after all, even within this small island there are other lake and mountain areas which have higher mountains and larger lakes – not that grandeur, beauty or even ruggedness are dependent upon size alone. Perhaps this is where the clue to the uniqueness of the Lake District lies. All the essential ingredients of a mountain landscape are there, but on a comparatively small scale, so that its grandeur seems friendly and welcoming rather than forbidding. Allied to this is another unique feature, the 'Englishness' of the region, which marks it off as different not only from the Scottish Highlands but even from nearby Snowdonia. From almost all the major Lakeland peaks you look down on peaceful, green, wooded valleys, which have a lushness that you might associate with gentler landscapes further south, and these are dotted with attractive villages, whose pubs and tearooms are a mecca for ramblers.

The Lake District is remarkably compact. From Grasmere, the approximate central point, nowhere is more than 20 miles (32km) away. Like the spokes of a wheel, a metaphor coined by Wordsworth himself, the Lakes radiate from this central hub. To the north-west are the twin lakes of Derwent Water and Bassenthwaite, either side of Keswick, and, a little to the south, the three adjoining lakes of Buttermere, Crummock Water and Loweswater. To the west lie the most inaccessible and therefore least visited of all the lakes, Ennerdale Water and Wast Water. Immediately to the south are Grasmere and Rydal Water, and beyond them Coniston Water and Windermere (England's longest lake), with the small Esthwaite Water lying in between. To the north-east, over the Kirkstone Pass, comes first the tiny Brothers Water and then the curving majesty of Ullswater. In addition to these there are the major reservoirs of Thirlmere and Hawcswater, as well as the countless tarns that form some of the most delightful features of the Lakeland landscape. Separating these lake-filled valleys – not forgetting that some of the most beautiful valleys in the Lake District (Langdale, Dunnerdale and Eskdale) are without lakes – are the dramatic hills and fells. Chief amongst these are the four 3000ft (915m) peaks – England's highest mountains (Scafell Pike, Sca Fell, Helvellyn and Skiddaw), followed by Great Gable, Pillar and many others that top the 2000ft (610m) mark.

Lakeland Towns

Along the eastern, landward frontier is a line of towns which have been the traditional gateways into the Lake District from the rest of the country: Lancaster, Kendal, Penrith and Carlisle. All the main lines of north-south communication pass either through or close to these. To the west, the main gateways from the coast are Cockermouth and Egremont. One feature common to all six of these 'gateway' towns is that they possess

the remains of medieval castles. Within in the Lakes themselves, the only real town for many centuries was Keswick, until Victorian tourism led to the expansion of Ambleside and what was virtually the creation of the resorts of Windermere and Bowness.

Ullswater seen from Glenridding

Geological Roots

The physical features of Lakeland are inevitably rooted in its geology. In simple terms there are three broad, roughly parallel bands of rock extending across the area from west to east. Oldest of these are the Skiddaw slates in the north which, though hard, have been eroded by weather over a long period of time to produce a landscape of relatively smooth and rounded hills, such as Blencathra and Skiddaw itself. Next comes the central zone of volcanic rocks, sometimes called the Borrowdale Series, which are highly weather-resistant. These have given rise to the spectacular craggy outline of the 'central massif', including Sca Fell, Great Gable, the Langdale Pikes, Coniston Old Man and Helvellyn. Lastly come the softer Silurian rocks of the southern band, the youngest rocks, stretching from Coniston Water across to Windermere and Kendal, and creating a gentler landscape than further north. Around the edges of these main bands are areas of limestone and sandstone and the coal measures that gave rise to the west coast industrial area around Workington and Whitehaven, and also outcrops of granite in Eskdale and elsewhere.

The Ice Age had the most striking effect on the landscape of the Lake District. As the glaciers moved outwards from the central fells, they scoured out and rounded the main valleys into their present U-shapes, leaving tributary 'hanging valleys' stranded high up on the sides, from which water cascades down in spectacular falls. At the same time, the glaciers also gouged out the depressions into which the lakes and tarns were formed and restricted their outlets by depositing debris called moraines. In some cases, the build-up of these moraines caused a single lake to be divided into two smaller ones, clearly seen at Keswick, which stands on low-lying ground between Bassenthwaite and Derwent Water (once one large lake) and also at Buttermere village, similarly placed between Buttermere and Crummock Water.

Celtic Resistance

With its damp climate, rugged terrain and comparatively thin soils, the Lake District was not one of the main centres of population in prehistoric Britain, but there are some monuments of this period, principally the spectacular Bronze Age stone circle at Castlerigg, near Keswick. The interest of the Romans in the area was purely military, and the Cumbrian coast became a logical western extension of Hadrian's Wall, with a line of forts stretching along it. Chief of these was Ravenglass, possibly intended as a base from which to launch an invasion of Ireland. From here the Romans drove a road through the heart of the Lake District via the Hardknott and Wrynose passes to the fort at Ambleside and thence along the High Street ridge, the line of which is now a magnificent footpath, to link up with their fort near Brougham. Along this route are remains of the Bath House at Ravenglass and the dramatically sited and impressive Hardknott Fort, which commands the head of Eskdale.

The collapse of Roman power was followed by several centuries of confusion, in which native Celts and successive waves of invaders, first Angles, and later Norsemen, struggled for supremacy. In its relative isolation, protected by natural mountain defences, the Lake District was one of the areas where, for a time, the Celts, as in the other western fastnesses of Wales and Cornwall, were able successfully to resist the penetration of the Angles from the south and east, maintaining the independent kingdom of Strathclyde, which straddled the present English-Scottish border and, at its greatest extent, stretched from the Ribble to the Clyde. The name 'Cumbria' in fact comes from the Celtic *cymry* meaning 'comrades' – the Welsh word for the Welsh.

Norse Influence

More successful invaders were the Norsemen, who moved into the area from the coast, coming via Ireland and the Isle of Man, and developed small farming communities in the remote western valleys. Norse influence on the region is still strong: in the common place-name ending -thwaite, in the use of Norse words to describe physical features – gill, beck, tarn and force – and in the Viking crosses at Gosforth and elsewhere.

Frontier Region

For centuries Cumbria was a debatable frontier region, claimed by both English and Scottish kings. This was why William the Conqueror did not include it in his 'Domesday' survey in 1086, and it was not until after his son William II captured

All the waters from Great Langdale squeeze through this narrow gap at Skelwith Force

Carlisle in 1092 and established a strong royal fortress there that the border was finally fixed. Other castles were built around the periphery of the Lake District at Cockermouth, Egremont, Kendal, Appleby, Lancaster, Brough and Brougham.

Following the Norman Conquest came the monastic orders, who also established their sites around the edge of, rather than actually within, the Lake District – at Holme Cultram, St Bees, Calder, Cartmel, Shap and Lanercost.
Most powerful and wealthy of these was the great foundation of Furness, whose abbots – because of the remoteness of the area from the main centres of power – enjoyed the status of almost independent sovereigns. These monasteries owned considerable land in the Lake District and played a major role in the economic development of the region: clearing woods, extending sheep-farming and exploiting its mineral resources, principally the iron ores of Furness.

However, Scottish incursions were frequent throughout the later Middle Ages. Apart from the construction of a new castle at Penrith, this is most obviously reflected in the building of small fortified towers or mini-castles called 'peel' towers. With the ending of the Scottish raids and the coming of more settled times, many of these peel towers were expanded to form the core of stately homes, as happened at Muncaster Castle, Dacre Castle and Levens Hall.

Drystone Walls, Sheep, Quarries and Mines

Agricultural prosperity came later to the Lake District than to most other parts of England but in the late 17th century it produced the same great rebuilding of farmhouses, and some fine examples exist of yeoman farmers' or statesmen's houses of the period, such as Town End, near Troutbeck. During the late 18th and early 19th centuries came the enclosure movement, when drystone walls spread from the valleys onto the open fells, creating one of the most striking man-made features on the Lakeland landscape.

Industrial activity in the area was at its height from the late 16th to the 19th century, especially woollen cloth manufacturing around Kendal and Hawkshead, the quarrying of granite and slate, and the mining of copper in Borrowdale and around Coniston, iron ore in Furness, and graphite ('wad' or 'plumbago') in Borrowdale, which gave rise to Keswick's famous pencil industry. Although the scars from these industries are gradually being grown over and hidden now, they still exist, and provide a fascinating field for industrial archaeologists. The most popular survival of Eskdale's granite-quarrying industry, however, is the narrow-gauge Ravenglass and Eskdale Railway, now a superb tourist attraction.

From Poetry to Tourism

Despite these developments, the Lake District remained a relatively little-known backwater until towards the end of the 18th century. Lakeland tourism was largely initiated by William Wordsworth and the other Lake Poets, who were among the foremost leaders of the Romantic movement, when there was an awakening interest in the wilder areas of Britain, previously shunned as being both barbaric and dangerous. Wordsworth is the greatest of all the many Lakeland literary figures and, unlike some of the others, was a native Cumbrian. Born at Cockermouth and educated at Hawkshead, he lived most of his life in the Lake District, especially around Grasmere and Rydal, where he spent the last fifty-one of his eighty years. Once his fame was established, he attracted a group of poets around him – Robert Southey, Samuel Taylor Coleridge and Thomas De Quincey, known collectively as the 'Lake Poets', and since their time a series of other varied literary figures have flocked into the Lake District to make temporary or permanent homes there, including Sir Walter Scott, Lord Tennyson, John Ruskin, Arthur Ransome, Beatrix Potter and Sir Hugh Walpole.

The predominantly intellectual and aristocratic early visitors were superseded both by middle-class industrialists, seeking hotels or homes in the country, and, once the railway reached both Windermere and Keswick around the middle of the 19th century and roads were improved, by working-class day-trippers. It is noteworthy that Wordsworth, largely the instigator of Lakeland tourism, vehemently opposed the extension of the railway from Windermere to his beloved Grasmere, exclaiming passionately, 'is there no nook of English ground secure from rash assault?'

Birthplace of Conservation

It was the growing commercial and industrial pressures on the Lake District – tourism, large-scale quarrying and, later on, demands for reservoirs and forestry – that brought forth the conservationist movements.

The Lake District Defence Society, forerunner of the Friends of the Lake District, was founded in 1883. Canon Rawnsley, Vicar of Crosthwaite, near Keswick, was one of the founders and main driving forces behind the National Trust (founded in 1895), whose earliest properties were acquired in the Lakes at Brandelhow, on the western side of Derwent Water, and Gowbarrow on the shores of Ullswater (where Wordsworth is alleged to have seen the daffodils that inspired the best-known poem in the English language). The National Trust now owns about 25 per cent of the area and it, together with the Friends of the Lake District, the Council for the Preservation of Rural England and other bodies continue to fight to conserve the area's natural environment.

Designation as a National Park
The designation of the Lake District as a National Park in 1951 was a conservation victory. Its boundaries encompass virtually the whole region, including a section of coastline roughly between Ravenglass and the Duddon estuary. Although this is England's only mountain region, it cannot be emphasised too strongly that the Lake District is not a walking area just for super-fit fell-walkers. Along with tough and challenging ascents, there are also plenty of middle- and lower-level walks, from which the views are just as varied and spectacular as from the higher points, and easy, attractive circuits of several of the lakes are possible, which make excellent half-day walks.

Walking in the Lake District is a pastime that can be enjoyed by people of all ages, all degrees of fitness and all interests. The Lake District is truly, as Wordsworth said, anticipating the later creation of the National Park, 'a sort of national property, in which every man has a right and an interest who has an eye to perceive and a heart to enjoy', and the best way to both perceive and enjoy it is to follow its extensive and varied footpaths.

The Lake District National Park is the largest of the country's National Parks. Its 885 sq mile (2292 sq km) area is best loved for the variety and contrast of its landscape. It is one of eleven National Parks in England and Wales. They were given this special status to protect their spectacular and fragile landscapes so that people could continue to enjoy and understand them.

National Parks cover almost 8 per cent of the English countryside. They are home to at least 168,000 people and visited by millions of others each year. The Lake District National Park is a celebration of how people and nature can work together. Although the Lake District countryside may seem wild, it looks the way it does because of human activity, particularly farming. People have been using the area for at least 10,000 years and in 1951 it was established as a National Park to protect it for future generations.

The land in the Lake District National Park is nearly all privately owned and much of it is farmed so it is important to use the Country Code:
• Enjoy the countryside and respect its life and work • Guard against all risk of fire • Fasten all gates • Keep your dogs under close control • Keep to public paths across farmland • Use gates and stiles to cross fences, hedges and walls • Leave livestock, crops and machinery alone • Take your litter home • Help to keep all water clean • Protect wildlife, plants and trees • Take special care on country roads.

Judith Quigley (Interpretation Projects Officer),
Lake District National Park Authority

Loweswater

Start	Loweswater
Distance	4 miles (6.4km)
Approximate time	2 hours
Parking	Parking-areas by the road at northern end of the lake
Refreshments	None *en route* but pub at Loweswater village close by
Ordnance Survey maps	Landranger 89 (West Cumbria), Outdoor Leisure 4 (The English Lakes – North Western area)

Loweswater, a small, quiet, relatively remote and little-known lake, is particularly attractive, surrounded by softer and greener scenery than some of its larger neighbours. This circuit of it makes an ideal leisurely walk, either on a hot day when strenuous activity does not appeal or when it is misty and there seems to be little point in going up on the high fells. On such a circuit the views are ever-changing and there is a striking contrast between the higher and more rugged fells that lie at the southern end of the lake and the gentler and lower hills at its northern end.

Much of the lower slopes of the fells around Loweswater are covered with woodland which is in the care of the National Trust, and most views across the lake towards its southern end are dominated by the conical-shaped Mellbreak (1676ft/512m), which lies between Loweswater and Crummock Water.

From the parking-area walk along the road, with the lake on the right; immediately there are fine views to be enjoyed across the lake to Holme Wood, on the opposite slopes, and beyond is the distinctive outline of Mellbreak. After about ¹/₂ mile (800m) turn right, at a footpath access sign, to the lakeshore and in a few yards turn left along a wooded path, parallel to and just below the road. If conditions are muddy or the water level is high, it will probably be more convenient, if less attractive, to

continue along the road.

The path later rejoins the road, and you keep along it for just over ¹/₂ mile (800m), turning right along a narrow lane at a sign 'Loweswater 1 mile' **A**. Mellbreak rears up abruptly in front, and to the left there is a glimpse of Crummock Water, backed by the bare, forbidding slopes of Grasmoor. Follow this lane down to a National Trust car park, go through a gate and continue along a broad path heading towards the lake. Ahead, looking up the lake, are much lower, gentler, greener hills, which gradually merge into the coastal lowlands.

Go through a series of gates, passing Watergate Farm on the left, and bear right by the foot of the lake to go through two more gates into the lovely Holme Wood. Keep along the lakeshore path through the wood, which contains

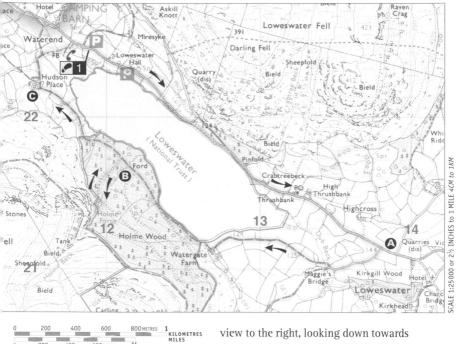

SCALE 1:25000 or 2½ INCHES to 1 MILE 4CM to 1KM

| 0 | 200 | 400 | 600 | 800 METRES | 1 |
| 0 | 200 | 400 | 600 YARDS | ½ | |

KILOMETRES
MILES

some fine old mature oak and ash trees, and from which there are most attractive views across the lake to Loweswater Fell. After crossing Holme Beck **B**, a short detour along a clear path to the left leads up to the impressive-looking Holme Force, the noise of which will be apparent long before you actually see it.

At the far end of the wood, pass through a gate and continue ahead over a stile, climbing gently. Climb another stile by a gate and turn right **C**, passing Hudson Place Farm on the left. Continue along a tarmac track heading downhill and, where the track bends sharply to the left, climb a stile ahead and walk across a field towards another stile. From here you get a final, superb

view to the right, looking down towards the far end of Loweswater, dominated by the peaks of Mellbreak and Grasmoor.

Climb the stile, keep ahead to another one, climb that and turn left up to a third stile a few yards ahead, which admits you to the road. Turn right, back to the parking-area. ●

Quiet and secluded Loweswater

Aira Force and Dockray

Start	Aira Force
Distance	3½ miles (5.6km)
Approximate time	1½ hours
Parking	National Trust car park at Aira Force
Refreshments	Café near car park, pub at Dockray
Ordnance Survey maps	Landranger 90 (Penrith, Keswick & Ambleside), Outdoor Leisure 5 (The English Lakes – North Eastern area)

This is a walk which, for remarkably little effort, provides both dramatic waterfall scenery and several outstanding views over Ullswater and the fells beyond. The paths are good throughout and there are no difficult or strenuous sections, making it ideal for walkers of all ages. But take care: the rocks look inviting and make excellent vantage points for admiring the falls but, in wet weather, they can become slippery.

Aira Force plunges through a wooded ravine

This walk is mainly on land owned by the National Trust, who have constructed good footpaths and who have provided footbridges over Aira Beck which make ideal viewing platforms for the falls. In fact, Aira Beck plunges over three falls in less than ½ mile (800m): first Aira Force, second High Force and finally a third, unnamed fall.

Begin by taking the path at the far end of the car park, go through a gate and keep ahead, turning right at another gate into woodland and down towards the beck. Do not cross the footbridge in front but turn left away from the main path along the left-hand side of the beck. Follow it up through the steep-sided, wooded ravine, passing the three falls in turn. This is a most attractive and dramatic walk, especially after rain, when the waters of the beck, confined within the narrow sides of the ravine, surge over the rocks. Do not cross any of the footbridges, except perhaps to view the falls and to take photographs, but keep along the same side of the beck all the while.

At the third and final fall, turn left through a gap in a wall **Ⓐ** and head across a field, keeping to the right of a group of rocks, to a gate **Ⓑ**. Go through and turn right along the road into the small village of Dockray. Cross the bridge, bear right and, opposite the Royal Hotel, turn right along a walled track at the public footpath sign for Aira Force and Ulcat Row **Ⓒ**. Bear right, pass through a gate and in front is a striking view of the rocky slopes of Gowbarrow Fell. Bear left past the farm, then bear right, go through a gate and continue ahead. Now comes an excellent view of Place Fell, in front, on the other side of Ullswater.

Head into the woods and through a gate to rejoin Aira Beck, continuing along the other side of the ravine past the three falls. There is a choice here between a higher or a lower path, but the higher one has the advantage of giving some superb views towards the head of Ullswater. Finally turn right over a footbridge to return to the car park. ●

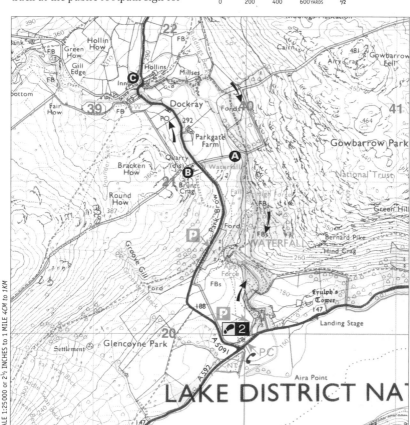

Stanley Force and Eskdale

Start	Dalegarth
Distance	4½ miles (7.2km)
Approximate time	2½ hours
Parking	Station car park at Dalegarth (charge), near Boot
Refreshments	Café at Dalegarth station, pub and restaurant at Boot
Ordnance Survey maps	Landrangers 89 (West Cumbria) and 96 (Barrow-in-Furness & South Lakeland), Outdoor Leisure 6 (The English Lakes – South Western area)

A dramatic waterfall, half-hidden in a tree-lined ravine, gentle riverside meadows, an old pack-horse bridge and an attractive isolated church are the chief ingredients of this interesting and varied walk amidst the glorious scenery of Eskdale. This is a short, easy walk, whose beauty can be enjoyed at any season of the year, but watch out for slippery conditions near the fall.

Eskdale is a long, narrow dale stretching from the foot of Scafell Pike down to the coast at Ravenglass. Although there is no lake, it is infinitely attractive and varied, and it is well endowed with footpaths, including both easy and more challenging ones.

Start by turning right out of the station car park along the road. Turn first left along a lane Ⓐ, cross the River Esk and keep ahead past a car park,

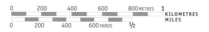

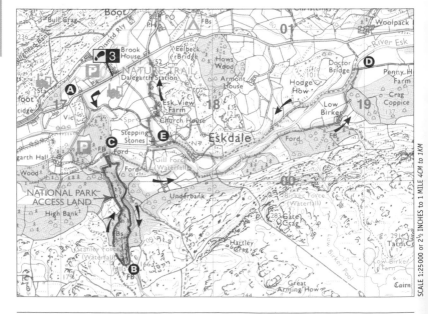

where the lane becomes a rough track. At a finger sign 'Waterfalls' and a public footpath sign for Stanley Ghyll and Birker Moor, turn left, go through a gate, bear left and keep ahead at a junction of paths by a wall on the left. Where the main path turns right, keep ahead through a gate, into the woods and bear right by the stream through Stanley Ghyll. Walk along the side of the narrow, rocky, thickly wooded gorge to a footbridge. Cross over and continue up the other side of the stream, soon recrossing it by a second footbridge and then going ahead up to a third footbridge **B**. Here there is a splendid view of the secluded Stanley Force, which drops 60ft (18m) down the side of the dale. Its name comes from the Stanley family, of nearby Dalegarth Hall; a trip to see the waterfall was a favourite excursion for visitors in Victorian times, attracted by the wild and romantic appearance of the ravine.

Retrace your steps a few yards but, instead of dropping down to the second bridge, keep ahead along an uphill path, climbing steps to the top of the ravine and turning sharp right at the junction away from the stream on the left. After a brief further spell of climbing, start descending through the woodland. Drop down to rejoin the main path and turn left. Where that path veers left (where the wood was entered earlier), keep ahead, looking out for a footbridge **C**.

Cross it and continue through a gate, along a field path, and over a stream, bearing right and left and keeping by a wall on the left. Now follow a clear, broad path for nearly 1½ miles (2.4km); a most attractive route which keeps above the river on the left, giving grand views up Eskdale. Where the path forks, bear left downhill, passing a farm, and continue to a bridge **D**. This is Doctor Bridge, a 17th-century pack-horse bridge, later widened by a local doctor

Boot church – a delightful setting by the River Esk

to accommodate his horse and trap.

Turn left over the bridge and left again, at a public footpath sign to St Catherine's Church. Climb a stile and follow a most attractive path along the other side of the Esk, bearing slightly away from the river at a fork, continuing above it and eventually dropping down to rejoin it near the church **E**. This plain, isolated building stands in an idyllic and tranquil position by the river, ½ mile (800m) from the nearest village, Boot. The reason it was built here was presumably because from here it could serve a wide area of both Eskdale and Wasdale, while at the same time it was relatively accessible by riverside paths and at a point where the Esk could be forded or crossed by stepping-stones. From here a 'corpse road' led over to Wasdale Head, whose church was not granted rights of burial until towards the end of the 19th century. Although a church has stood on this site since probably the 12th century, the present structure is largely the result of rebuilding carried out in 1881.

At the church turn right along a walled track, keep ahead at a fork, bear right towards a farm and then bear left up to the road. Turn left back to the car park at Dalegarth Station. ●

Dodd Wood and Bassenthwaite

Start	Dodd Wood
Distance	3 miles (4.8km)
Approximate time	1½ hours
Parking	Mirehouse car park
Refreshments	Café at car park
Ordnance Survey maps	Landrangers 89 (West Cumbria) and 90 (Penrith, Keswick & Ambleside), Outdoor Leisure 4 (The English Lakes – North Western area)

A short but most attractive walk, ideal for a drowsy summer afternoon or an autumn morning. Initially the route climbs through Dodd Wood, part of Thornthwaite Forest, above Bassenthwaite Lake and along the lower slopes of Skiddaw, and then drops down across fields to a small church in an exquisite setting on the shores of the lake. Near the end of the walk you pass Mirehouse, where the house and grounds merit exploration.

Thornthwaite Forest comprises a number of Forestry Commission plantations, mostly on the western side of Bassenthwaite but including Dodd Wood on the eastern side. In the car park cross the footbridge by the side of the Old Sawmill, now a café and information centre, turn right and, in a few yards, turn sharp left up some steps to join a forest road. In a few yards this forest road heads down to the main road, but bear right, along an uphill path through tall conifers, with glimpses on the left through the trees over Bassenthwaite. Keep along the grassy path parallel with the road below, which continues climbing below the crags of Ullock Pike on the right and emerges at the top edge of the woods. From here there is a magnificent view over the lake, with the massed ranks of the high fells on the western edge of

Derwent Water (looking towards Keswick) making a striking contrast with the much gentler country on the right (looking towards the Cumbrian coast). Drop down into the woods again and, at a path junction, bear right along an uphill path, soon reaching another junction of paths **Ⓐ**.

Here turn sharp left, downhill through the trees to the road. Climb a stile, turn right along the road for just over 100 yds (91m) and, at a public footpath sign, turn sharp left down some steps **Ⓑ**. Passing a cottage on the left, go through a metal gate and keep ahead across the middle of a field to a gate. Go through and across the next field, heading towards a line of trees, continuing over a stile and along a path ahead through the trees to another gate. Pass through two gates in quick succession, head straight across a field

SCALE 1:25 000 or 2½ INCHES to 1 MILE 4CM to 1KM

0	200	400	600	800 METRES	1
0	200	400	600 YARDS	½	

KILOMETRES
MILES

This is one of the few churches dedicated to St Bega, who was the daughter of an Irish chief who fled to England, allegedly landing at nearby St Bees Head, also named after her.

While by the lakeshore, it is worthwhile noting that Bassenthwaite is, technically speaking, the only lake to be found in the Lake District; all the rest are either waters (eg Derwent Water and Ullswater) or meres (eg Windermere and Grasmere). Just before reaching the church, the route continues by bearing left along a path by the edge of Highfield Wood **C**, heading towards Mirehouse. In the background there is a fine view of the steeply wooded, distinctive, conical-shaped peak of Dodd (1647ft/502m). Go through a gate and keep ahead between trees and hedges towards the house, bearing right along a broad path that skirts the right-hand edge of the grounds. In the 19th century, Mirehouse was owned by the Spedding family, and Thomas and James Spedding (brothers) acquired a reputation for their hospitality, regularly entertaining some of the leading literary giants of the day. Among those who stayed here were Thomas Carlyle, Edward Fitzgerald and Lord Tennyson, and the lonely lakeside setting of St Bega's Church was supposed to have inspired the latter's description of the death of King Arthur in his poem *Morte d'Arthur*. The house, mainly built in the 17th century but subsequently enlarged, faithfully re-creates the atmosphere of the 19th century when it was a literary mecca, with many portraits and mementos of the people who stayed here. It stands in a superb position between the lake and the wooded slopes of Dodd, and has most attractive grounds.

The path turns right by the house and continues straight ahead to the road opposite the car park. ●

to yet another gate, go through that and continue across the next field to a gate and road. Go straight across, through a gate opposite, signposted to St Bega's Church, and keep ahead by a wall on the right.

From this path the views ahead of the Derwent Fells and the thickly wooded slopes of Thornthwaite Forest on both sides of the lake are superb. Where the main track bears left, keep ahead, go through a gate and continue across meadows down towards the church by the lakeshore, later rejoining the main track. St Bega's Church is the church for Bassenthwaite, though the village is nearly 3 miles (4.8km) to the north. It is an exquisite little building, dating mostly from the 12th and 13th centuries, whose beauty and air of tranquillity are enhanced by its remote and idyllic setting by the lake. Although heavily restored in the Victorian period, it retains its fine Norman chancel arch.

Thirlmere and Great How

Start	Station Coppice car park on eastern shore of Thirlmere
Distance	4 miles (6.4km)
Approximate time	2½ hours
Parking	Station Coppice car park (if full, another car park can be found almost opposite)
Refreshments	None
Ordnance Survey maps	Landranger 90 (Penrith, Keswick & Ambleside), Outdoor Leisure 5 (The English Lakes – North Eastern area)

In some ways Thirlmere is the Cinderella of the English Lakes; when driving past it along the Ambleside–Keswick road, it appears to be surrounded by thick conifers, which make it seem gloomy and uninteresting, while it is also neglected and looked down on because it is an artificial lake. This walk, however, much of which is on newly created, well-surfaced and well-waymarked permissive paths, is certainly not gloomy, while the woodland passed through in the first part of the walk is mixed and most attractive and, both from the summit of Great How and on the return route along the side of the valley, there are grand views over the lake and the encircling fells.

Thirlmere came into being towards the end of the 19th century, when Manchester Corporation built a dam and raised the water-level in the valley by more than 50ft (15m). As a result, two villages and several outlying farms were submerged, and two existing small lakes were joined up and expanded to create a ¾-mile (1.2km) long reservoir, which was completed in 1892. A vigorous campaign was fought to prevent such desecration, spearheaded by the leading conservationists of the day, including John Ruskin, but to no avail. This failure was not without its positive side, however, as what had happened at Thirlmere, together with concern over similar threats to the landscape, provided the impetus for the formation of the National Trust in 1895.

At the car park go down the steps and turn left through a gate, at a permissive path sign to Legburthwaite and Great How. Follow a grassy path ahead down towards the lake, joining a stream on the left and keeping by it to a gate. Go through and continue down through the trees, bearing right at a footpath sign along a path through the tall conifers just above the lakeshore **Ⓐ**. The route is easy to follow, by or just above the lake, waymarked with white arrows.

After a mile (1.6km) a footpath sign at a path junction is reached **Ⓑ**. Here take the path ahead, signposted Great How, which winds steeply through more mixed woodland to the top . Although encircled and partially obscured by conifers, there is still a fine view from the summit: northwards over Thirlmere towards Keswick, with Raven Crag standing out prominently in the foreground and eastwards to the Helvellyn range. Retrace your steps from the tree-encircled summit back to the junction of paths **B**, turn left (signposted Legburthwaite and Keswick) and take the track along the edge of Greathow Wood. This track drops downhill, turns left and continues parallel to the main road, with a striking view of Castle Rock on the right. Eventually the track bears right, through a gate and on to the road **D**.

Cross over, turn right along the road for about 100 yds (91m) and then turn left over a stile at a public footpath sign. Walk along the edge of a field, following the wall round to the left to a gate. Go through, turn right along the road through Legburthwaite and, by some houses, turn left at a bridleway sign for Glenridding via Sticks Pass **E**. Follow a tarmac track uphill to a ladder-stile, climb over, continue up to a stile by a gate, climb over that and keep ahead, still uphill, to go through a gate by Beck Fall.

Bear right over the fall, bear left to a footpath sign and bear right again along the permissive path to Grasmere via Swirls. The path climbs to a wall corner and then follows left-hand side of the wall along the valley, with an excellent view of Great How on the right. Nearing a group of trees on the right, the path bears slightly left, away from the wall, keeping above the trees and crossing a footbridge over Fisherplace Ghyll, an impressive sight.

Bear left to a wall corner and again keep along the left-hand edge of the wall. At a junction of paths by a beck, leave the wall, which bends to the right, and keep straight ahead along a clearly defined path, still following the side of

SCALE 1:25000 or 2½ INCHES to 1 MILE 4CM :o 1KM

0 200 400 600 800 METRES
0 200 400 600 YARDS ½

1 KILOMETRES
MILES

the valley. From this path there are fine views over Thirlmere, which clearly show that with the passage of time its edges have become softened and it has now lost much of its artificiality. The path gradually bears right and starts descending to meet a wall, keeping by the wall downhill to a footbridge by a waterfall. Cross it and continue to a T-junction of paths by the edge of a wood **F**. Turn right, go through a gate and follow a path by a beck to a second gate. Go through that, over a footbridge and turn right through a car park. Walk straight across the grassy knoll ahead down to a gate, and the starting point is on the other side of the main road. ●

Back of Bowness

Start	Bowness-on-Windermere
Distance	4 miles (6.4km)
Approximate time	2½ hours
Parking	Bowness
Refreshments	Plenty of pubs, restaurants and cafés in Bowness
Ordnance Survey maps	Landranger 96 (Barrow-in-Furness & South Lakeland), Outdoor Leisure 7 (The English Lakes – South Eastern area)

The rather urban surroundings of Bowness, on the eastern shores of Windermere, do not at first glance seem a promising place for rural walks, but it is surprising how quickly you can escape into a peaceful pastoral environment, as this pleasant, half-day walk rapidly reveals. Soon after the start and just before the finish of the walk, there are two prominent crags that give outstanding views across Windermere to the more rugged terrain beyond.

Despite a 15th-century church and some old houses, Bowness is principally a creation of the Victorian tourist boom, when the coming of the railway in 1847 brought visitors in ever-increasing numbers into the area. Windermere Town, which grew up around the rail terminal, and Bowness were formerly quite separate places, but the expansion of both in the late 19th century caused them to become merged into one. Large, ornate hotels were built to cater for the influx of tourists and steamboat services enabled them to cruise up and down Windermere, enjoying the scenery in comfort. Bowness is still one of the most popular towns in the Lake District, offering a wide variety of sporting and leisure activities and a range of restaurants, pubs, hotels and cafés to suit every requirement.

The walk begins at the bottom end of the town near the lakeside. Walk up the main road in the direction of Windermere Town, and turn right along Helm Road. Passing the large Windermere Hydro Hotel on the left, continue ahead, climbing steadily to reach the Biskey Howe viewpoint, a slight detour off the road to the left. From here, only a short distance from the bustle of the town, is a glorious view over Windermere and a convenient view-indicator shows the vast array of familiar peaks that can be seen from this point. Continue along a tarmac drive past houses, keeping ahead after the drive becomes a rough track. Walk past a farm on the right and, where the main track bends right, turn left through a gate **Ⓐ**, cross a small field to another gate, go through and keep ahead towards some modern houses. Climb a stone stile and continue ahead, turning right along a path between a hedge and wire fence and heading uphill to a footpath sign. Turn sharp right, bear left through a gate by

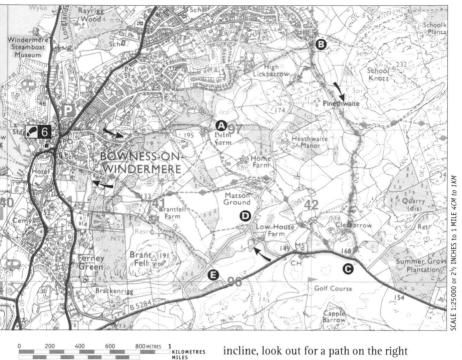

SCALE 1:25000 or 2½ INCHES to 1 MILE 4CM to 1KM

the side of a house and continue ahead, climbing gently all the while across the field to another gate. Go through, cross a lane to a stone stile, climb that and keep ahead along the edge of a field down to a ladder-stile.

Climb over, cross a footbridge, walk up some steps ahead and turn right along a tarmac track **B**. Where that track bends right, keep ahead through a gate, cross a field to another gate, go through that, cross a stream and continue straight ahead. In this quiet, green, well-wooded landscape, the noise and crowds of Bowness could be miles away. Keep along the track through several gates, past farm buildings and ahead to a road **C**

Turn right, keep ahead (ignoring a Dales Way footpath sign on the right) past the Windermere Golf Club and turn right along a narrow lane signposted to Heathwaite. At a junction **D**, turn left along a pleasantly undulating wooded lane and, at the bottom of a slight incline, look out for a path on the right leading up to some stone steps and a metal gate **E**. Go through and follow a path ahead which winds up the right-hand side of Brant Fell. At Brantfell Farm keep to the left and proceed uphill and onto the brow with the wall close on the right. Climb a stile and head downhill, between the wall and the fence protecting newly planted trees. At the bottom climb a stone stile, slightly to the left in the wall facing you, and continue to the promontory of Post Knott straight ahead for the finest view of the walk: a magnificent panorama up and down Windermere, with the thickly wooded Claife Heights on the other side of the lake and Wetherlam, Coniston Old Man, the Langdale Pikes and other peaks standing out prominently on the horizon.

Turn right down to a gate, go through and turn left along a winding, wooded downhill path. Just before a wall, turn left through a gate, head across a field to another gate, go through that and along the road ahead back to the centre of Bowness. ●

Elterwater and Skelwith Bridge

Start	Elterwater
Distance	6 miles (9.7km)
Approximate time	3 hours
Parking	Elterwater village. Alternative parking-areas on common land just north of the village
Refreshments	Pub at Elterwater, pub and café at Skelwith Bridge
Ordnance Survey maps	Landranger 90 (Penrith, Keswick & Ambleside), Outdoor Leisure 7 (The English Lakes – South Eastern area)

This is mainly a low-level walk, with just a few modest climbs, through a pleasant landscape of fields, woods and waterfalls at the lower end of the two Langdales. Two waterfalls are passed and towards the end is a classic Lake District view, looking across Elter Water to the distinctive outline of the Langdale Pikes.

The pleasant Langdale village of Elterwater lies scattered around a small green beside Great Langdale Beck on the edge of open common land. Just to the east is the lake of the same name, a small reedy lake whose name comes from the Norse word *elptar* meaning 'swan', hence 'lake of the swans', an apt name, as it is still regularly visited by whooper swans from Siberia. The walk begins by crossing the bridge over the beck and taking the Coniston road. By the Eltermere Hotel on the left, turn right along a narrow lane **Ⓐ** and keep ahead, climbing quite steeply up what soon becomes a stony track. The track climbs past woodland, emerging into more open country at the top, where there is a superb view ahead over Little Langdale to the Coniston Fells.

At this point, turn left off the main track through a gate **Ⓑ** and walk across a field, dropping down to a stone stile. Climb it, keep ahead to another one, climb that and continue along the edge of a field, dropping into Little Langdale. Go through a farmyard, continue to a road, turn left along it for a short distance and then turn right through a gate **Ⓒ**, at a public footpath sign; continue downhill to a footbridge over the River Brathay. Cross over, keep straight ahead to a stile, climb that and continue uphill to Stang End Farm **Ⓓ**.

Turn left past the house along a tarmac lane, with lovely views on the left of the wooded valley of the Brathay and the fells behind. At a farm keep ahead through the farmyard (where the tarmac lane bends right), bear right through a waymarked gate at the end, head across to a second gate, go through and keep by a wall on the left to a third gate. Pass through that into the beautiful Colwith Woods and at a path junction take the left-hand fork downhill towards the river. Follow its banks to Colwith Force, a delightful fall set in woodland, where the Brathay drops about 40ft (12m). Continue by the

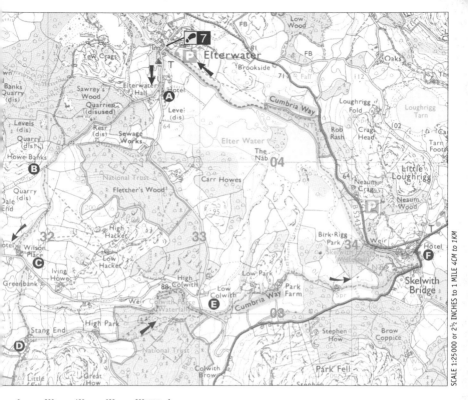

SCALE 1:25000 or 2½ INCHES to 1 MILE 4CM to 1KM

```
0      200    400    600    800 METRES  1
                                        KILOMETRES
                                        MILES
0      200    400    600 YARDS   ½
```

river through the woods to a road **E**.

Turn right and, after about 100 yds (91m), cross a beck and turn left over a stone stile at a public footpath sign for Skelwith Bridge. Cross a field, heading towards some trees, climb a stile and head steeply up through the woods. Climb another stile at the top and, with glorious views of Great Langdale in front, follow the path ahead up to a farm. Go through a gate, over the farm track, over a fence opposite and continue ahead to a stile. Climb it, keep ahead to another stile, climb that and continue to Park Farm, passing through the middle of the farm buildings. Keep ahead, bear right at a public footpath sign, and follow a winding path past another farm, bearing left at a fork in the paths by a tree and continuing down through woods to a gate. A few yards ahead, turn left down the road into Skelwith Bridge.

Cross the bridge and immediately turn left at a public footpath sign to Elterwater **F**. Walk past the showroom of the Kirkstone Slate Galleries, through the middle of the quarry yard, where the locally quarried green slate is processed and sold, and keep ahead along a riverside path. Soon you come to Skelwith Force, where a viewing platform is provided. Here the river narrows and falls 16ft (5m) over a rocky ledge; although the fall is not high it is most impressive as the combined waters from Great and Little Langdale surge through this narrow gap. Keep along the riverside path, go through a gate and continue across meadows, by the shores of Elter Water and through woods, keeping in a virtually straight line back to Elterwater village. The path is easy to follow and there are spectacular views of the Langdale Pikes, especially from the lakeshore, where the sight of the twin pikes is one of the truly memorable Lakeland views. ●

Hawkshead and Tarn Hows

Start	Hawkshead
Distance	6 miles (9.7km)
Approximate time	3 hours
Parking	Hawkshead
Refreshments	Pubs and cafés in Hawkshead
Ordnance Survey maps	Landrangers 90 (Penrith, Keswick & Ambleside) and 96 (Barrow-in-Furness & South Lakeland), Outdoor Leisure 7 (The English Lakes – South Eastern area)

A walk which links a picture-postcard village and a picture-postcard viewpoint can hardly fail to be attractive. From Hawkshead an easy-paced route proceeds across fields and through woods, climbing gently to a superb vantage point overlooking Tarn Hows. The return to Hawkshead is at a higher level, giving distant glimpses of Windermere and Esthwaite Water backed by green hillsides and rugged fells.

The combination of squares and narrow alleys, white-washed buildings, old inns and teashops, all overlooked by the sturdy-looking 15th-century church and surrounded by fells, makes Hawkshead the most picturesque village in the Lake District. Wordsworth was sent to be educated at the old Grammar School here between 1779 and 1787 and, while there, he lodged at Anne Tyson's cottage nearby. Hawkshead may be a village in size but its centre resembles that of a small market town.

From the car park make your way up to the main street and take the path on the left-hand side of the church, signposted to Tarn Hows and Coniston. Walk through the churchyard and continue along the path ahead, from where there is a lovely view of the church and the village huddled below it, with an impressive array of peaks beyond. Go through a gate, bear right at a footpath sign and head across a field

to another gate. Go through that, keep ahead through another gate and, on joining a tarmac lane, turn left and almost immediately right, through a gate at a public footpath sign to Tarn Hows and Coniston.

Walk straight across a field, bearing left uphill at a footpath sign **Ⓐ** to a gate, pass through and continue ahead, skirting a wood on the left. Go through a gate and along a path, with woodland, stream and waterfall on the right and, bearing right over the stream, proceed to another gate. Pass through it and head in a straight line across a field. Continue over a farm track and keep ahead, dropping down to a gate and public footpath sign where you join a road **Ⓑ**. Walk along the road, turn first right, signposted Tarn Hows, keep ahead at a junction and, shortly afterwards, turn left over a ladder-stile **Ⓒ**.

From here to Tarn Hows is all protected by the National Trust and

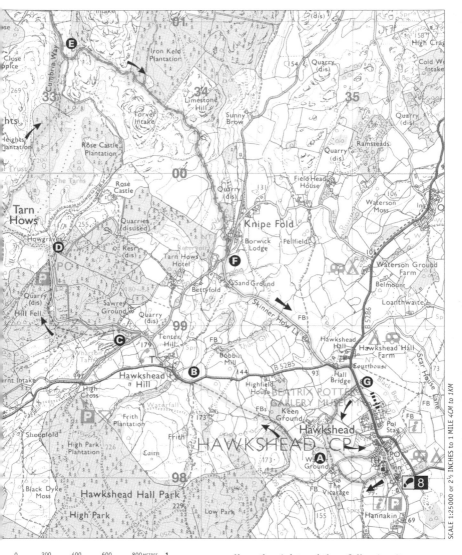

| 0 | 200 | 400 | 600 | 800 METRES | 1 |
| 0 | 200 | 400 | 600 YARDS | ½ | |

KILOMETRES
MILES

their footpaths are a pleasant alternative to staying on the road. After climbing the stile, turn right along a waymarked path that keeps by a wall, roughly parallel with the road on the right. Climb another ladder-stile and head uphill, making for a wall corner where there are two ladder-stiles close together. Climb the one on the right (National Trust sign for Tarn Hows) and enter woodland, drawing closer to the

wall on the right and then following it around to the right, climbing steadily. Gaps in the trees on the left reveal fine views over Coniston Water and the Old Man. Continue through the wood, and the path comes out onto the road **D**. Bear left over the brow and ahead is the classic view over Tarn Hows which adorns so many thousands of calendars and birthday cards. It certainly is a magnificent scene, with the tarn studded with small islands and surrounded by woods, and, behind, the rugged majesty of the Langdale Fells.

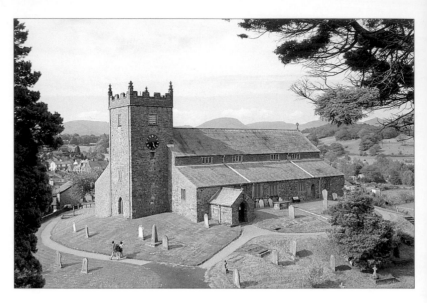

Hawkshead church occupies a ledge above this most picturesque of all Lakeland villages

Despite the great natural beauty of this scene, it is in fact partially man-made; most of the trees around the tarn are alien conifers and the raising of the water level by a dam caused what was originally several smaller tarns to become merged into one. However, such knowledge in no way impairs its attractiveness.

Continue downhill across the grass to go around the near end of the lake, and turn right through a gate along the lakeside path. Where the paths fork, bear left along the uphill one, through woodland and then ahead into open country, soon bearing right and dropping down to a stile. Climb over and turn right, along a steep, winding, walled track **E**. Soon the track levels out, and you follow it for 1¼ miles (2km). The advantages of the short, steep climb now become apparent; all the way there are fine and extensive views over Wetherlam, the Langdale Pikes, Tarn Hows and, later on, Ambleside, Windermere and Esthwaite Water.

Eventually the track drops down to a road **F**. Here keep straight ahead

(signposted Hawkshead) along a narrow lane opposite, Skinner How Lane, to another road. Turn left, head downhill and, at a T-junction, turn right. Just to the left is the 15th-century Hawkshead Courthouse, once part of a large manor owned by the monks of Furness Abbey. Keep along the road for about 200 yds (183m) and, just before a large house, turn right at a public footpath sign **G** along a tarmac drive by a stream on the right.

A more direct way back to Hawkshead is to keep along the road, but the suggested route is pleasanter and only marginally lengthier.

When the buildings of Hawkshead come into view on the left, look out for a metal gate on the left. Pass through it, turn right at a yellow waymark and follow a succession of these waymarks across a field, through a gate and across the next field, heading uphill to a footpath sign **A**. Here bear left and head towards a gate in a fence which admits you to a lane. Turn left along the lane for the short distance into Hawkshead.

Grasmere and Rydal Water

Start	Grasmere
Distance	5½ miles (8.9km)
Approximate time	3 hours
Parking	Grasmere
Refreshments	Pubs, restaurants and cafés in Grasmere
Ordnance Survey maps	Landranger 90 (Penrith, Keswick & Ambleside), Outdoor Leisure 7 (The English Lakes – South Eastern area)

Wordsworth was an outstanding walker, as well as a great poet. His walks took him all over the Lake District but, as he lived for most of his life around Grasmere and Rydal, we can assume that this walk covers some of the paths and scenery most familiar to him. It is an easy circuit around the adjoining lakes of Grasmere and Rydal Water which passes two of his homes and starts at the village where he lies buried and which he thought 'the loveliest spot that man hath ever found'.

Nowadays Grasmere is perhaps too thronged with tourists to be regarded as the idyllic village it seemed in Wordsworth's time but it is undeniably an attractive place in a superb setting. The simple 13th-century church in the centre of the village, 'of rude and antique majesty', is noted for its heavy pillars and exposed roof rafters. Wordsworth and many of the members of his family lie buried in the church-yard, and on one side of it is a tiny building, dating from 1687, which used to be the village schoolroom in Wordsworth's day but is now used for making and selling that most celebrated of local delicacies, Grasmere gingerbread.

In the village centre start by walking along Stock Lane, past the church, to the main road **Ⓐ**. Cross over, take the lane opposite and Dove Cottage is a few yards along on the left.

It was in 1799 that Wordsworth moved into Dove Cottage, a 17th-century former inn, with his sister Dorothy, and he lived here for the next nine years. It was here that he produced his finest poetry, here he married Mary Hutchinson, a local girl he had known for some years, and it was here that his first three children were born.

Lack of space caused the Wordsworths to move out in 1808 to larger premises, and his friend and fellow poet De Quincey took over the tenancy and lived there for the next twenty-seven years. In 1890, Dove Cottage was given to the Wordsworth Trust, who still own and maintain it together with an adjoining coach-house, which was opened as the Grasmere and Wordsworth Museum in 1981.

Continue up the lane past Dove Cottage and, where it bears right, continue ahead along an uphill track, following it around to the right, where it soon levels out. Now keep along an undulating path, which is easy to follow and fairly straight, at least after the first $^1/_2$ mile (800m), for $1^1/_2$ miles (2.4km) to Rydal, partly across meadows and partly through woodland, below the steep, forbidding crags of Nab Scar. The woods here are particularly attractive and there are lovely views through the trees on the right over Rydal Water. At a T-junction near some houses **B**, turn right, down into Rydal village.

On the right is Rydal Mount, the second Wordsworth residence passed on this walk. The most striking difference between here and Dove Cottage is that it is a much grander house: a reflection of Wordsworth's increased affluence and status. He moved here in 1813 and remained here until his death in 1850 at the age of eighty. It is still owned by one of his descendants, and inside are books, pictures and many family possessions. A little further down the road is the early 19th-century Rydal

church and behind it the wooded hillside of Dora's Field, bought by Wordsworth for his favourite daughter and named after her. In springtime it is a riot of daffodils.

Continue down the lane to the busy main road, cross over, turn left and shortly afterwards right over Pelter Bridge, an old packhorse bridge over the River Rothay **C**. Turn right again along a tarmac lane, past a small car park, climbing steadily. Past the last of the houses the lane degenerates into a rough track, which

Wordsworth is buried in the churchyard at Grasmere

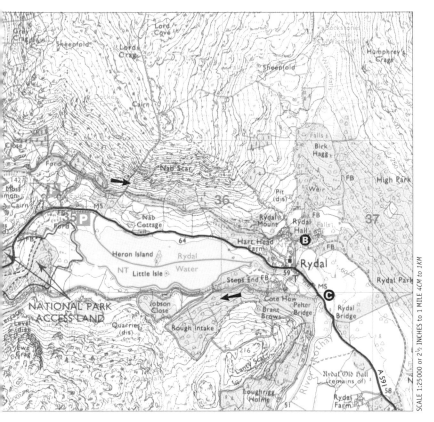

continues through woodland, eventually emerging onto the open fellside.

Where the path forks, bear left along the higher path, which continues above Rydal Water, and later the River Rothay, past caves and through disused quarries, giving grand views across the lake to Nab Scar and Rydal Fell beyond. At the next junction of paths, take the middle route, which keeps along a ledge above Grasmere and below the summit of Loughrigg Fell. This is Loughrigg Terrace, and the view from it over Grasmere lake and village, backed by Helm Crag, is justifiably one of the best-known and most beautiful of Lakeland scenes. Helm Crag is sometimes referred to as the 'Lion and the Lamb' as, from certain angles, its shape resembles a lion lying down by a lamb. Continue along the terrace to the end and, just before reaching a belt of woodland

ahead, turn right **D** down one of the steep, grassy paths to the lakeshore. Here turn left and follow a path through the woods, pass through a gate and continue across meadows, keeping close to the edge of the lake all the while. Climb a stile, and shortly afterwards the path veers left **E** up to a road. Turn right and keep along the narrow, winding road for ¾ mile (1.2km) back to Grasmere village.

If this walk is like a Wordsworth pilgrimage, the most appropriate way of finishing it must be to pay your respects at the poet's tomb; just a simple stone in the churchyard of the village amidst the mountains and lakes that he loved and which inspired some of the finest poetry in the English language. ●

Borrowdale

Start	Seatoller
Distance	7 miles (11.3km)
Approximate time	3½ hours
Parking	Seatoller
Refreshments	Cafés at Seatoller and Grange
Ordnance Survey maps	Landrangers 89 (West Cumbria) and 90 (Penrith, Keswick & Ambleside), Outdoor Leisure 4 (The English Lakes – North Western area)

Many have claimed that Borrowdale is the loveliest valley in England. Such accolades are, of course, always a matter of personal opinion but it must rank high on any list, and this walk, which reveals much of Borrowdale's exceptional beauty, certainly reinforces the claim. It also proves that it is not necessary to scale great heights in order to enjoy some of the finest Lakeland scenery. This is a low-level walk throughout – initially along the side of the valley and later returning along the banks of the Derwent – which has spectacular views of lakes, mountains, valleys, woods and river all the way.

The walk begins at the hamlet of Seatoller, lying near the head of Borrowdale and at the foot of the Honister Pass. Many of its cottages were built to house quarry workers and slate has been quarried nearby continuously since the 17th century.

Turn right out of the car park and walk through the hamlet in the direction of the Honister Pass. Where the road bends left Ⓐ keep ahead, climbing up to a gate at a public footpath sign. Go through and take the path ahead, which climbs quite steeply, curves to the right, crosses a wide track and heads up to a gate in a wall. Pass through that and bear right, keeping by a wall on the right. Soon the view ahead becomes dominated by the twin, wooded heights of Castle Crag and King's How on either side of the valley.

Cross a footbridge and continue ahead (still by a wall on the right), high above the village of Rosthwaite, which can be seen in the valley below. Cross a second footbridge, go through a gate, over a stile and a third footbridge, heading towards Castle Crag all the time. The path skirts the left-hand edge of the 980ft- (300m) high crag and starts to descend; ahead is a fine view down Borrowdale, opening out at the foot of Derwent Water.

Follow the path downhill, below the almost vertical slopes of the crag, through a gate and into woodland, to the banks of the River Derwent at an exceptionally idyllic spot called Bowder Dub Ⓑ. Here the river flows serenely between wooded banks, the whole scene dominated by King's How. Continue through the trees by a wall on the right, gradually bearing left away from the river. Near the end of the wooded area where the paths fork, bear left, following the bottom edge of a wooded cliff, first below the towering crags of High Spy and later the smoother flanks of Maiden Moor. Bear right, pass through a farm and keep ahead to a wall. Here turn right through a gate and climb the small hillock in front, where a stone seat commemorates the gift of the surrounding land to the National Trust in 1917 by Canon Rawnsley, one of the founders of the Trust. Drop down to a gate, go through and turn right **C** along a lane into Grange. This highly attractive village, distinguished by its picturesque bridge over the Derwent, gets its name from having been a grange, that is to say a granary or storehouse, of Furness Abbey, which owned much of Borrowdale.

Just past the church, turn right at a public bridleway sign to Honister, Rosthwaite and Seatoller **D**, along a track past cottages and ahead through trees, briefly rejoining the earlier part of the route as far as Bowder Dub **B**. Here take the path signposted to Rosthwaite and follow it up to a gate and stile. Go through and continue along a

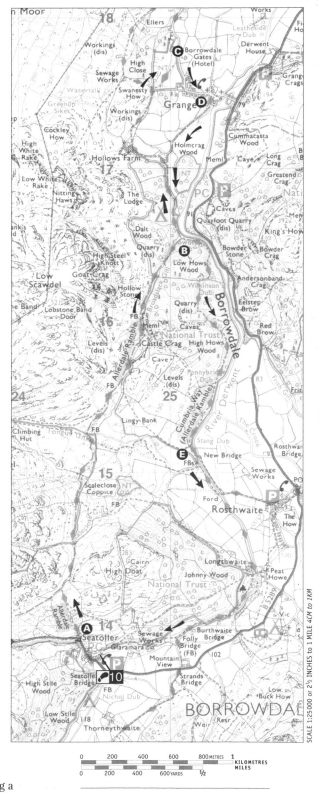

SCALE 1:25000 or 2½ INCHES to 1 MILE 4CM to 1KM

```
0    200   400   600   800 METRES   1
                                      KILOMETRES
                                      MILES
0    200   400   600 YARDS    ½
```

delightful woodland path, with the river below on the left, and King's How towering above the opposite bank. Soon the path climbs and bears away from the river, later dropping down to rejoin it and winding all the time amongst wooded rocky crags. Look out for a yellow waymark which indicates a sharp left-hand turn, past old quarry remains. The valley is thickly wooded and narrow here, hemmed in by Castle Crag on the right and King's How on the left but later, approaching Rosthwaite, it broadens out and becomes more open.

Emerging from the woods, go through a gate, keep ahead to rejoin the Derwent, and go through another gate to a footbridge **E**. Do not cross this footbridge but continue along a permissive path by the river to Long-thwaite Youth Hostel. Pass in front of the hostel and keep ahead by the river for a little while longer, before bearing right, away from it and following a path along the edge of Johnny Wood, a superb example of the oak woods which once covered the Lakeland valleys. From this path there are fine views ahead looking towards Seathwaite and the dramatic array of peaks massed at the head of Borrowdale. At the end of the wood, go through a gate, bear left and head in a straight line towards Seatoller, finally bearing left again at a gate and stile to the car park. ●

Bowder Dub – an idyllic spot by the Derwent

Cartmel and Hampsfield Fell

Start	Cartmel
Distance	7 miles (11.3km)
Approximate time	4 hours
Parking	Cartmel
Refreshments	Pubs and cafés in Cartmel
Ordnance Survey maps	Landranger 97 (Kendal & Morecambe), Outdoor Leisure 7 (The English Lakes – South Eastern area)

Most visitors to the Lake District hurry along the main roads to the high fells of the north and west or make for the busy resorts of Bowness, Ambleside and Keswick without realising that on the southern fringes of the national park lies a delightful village which possesses an ancient priory and which is surrounded by hills that provide good walking country, even if less energetic or spectacular than that to be found further north. This walk, in the gentle countryside around Cartmel, lying between the Lakeland mountains and Morecambe Bay, includes an easy climb to the summit of Hampsfield Fell which, though only 727ft (222m) high, gives splendid views over coastline and mountains.

Situated in an idyllic position amidst green wooded hills, in the valley of the little River Eea and not far from the coast, Cartmel is an enchanting old village of mainly 17th- and 18th-century grey stone cottages and narrow streets and alleys, centered on the square and dominated, inevitably, by the grand priory church. The village almost certainly grew up around the small Augustinian priory founded in 1190.

Being in such a remote area, Cartmel Priory enjoyed a largely uneventful history until its dissolution in 1537. Even then the destruction was not as complete as that suffered by other monasteries. Although the domestic buildings were demolished (no doubt quite a few of the local cottages were built with stones taken from these buildings), the church survived because part of it, the south choir aisle, or Town Choir, had been used as the parish church and was bought by the parishioners.

The most striking external feature of the priory is the unusual tower. When it was heightened in the 15th century, the extension was built diagonally to the original tower, giving it a highly distinctive, two-tiered appearance. Inside, notice the superb 15th-century east window and the intricate carvings of the medieval choir stalls with their elaborate 17th-century screens.

Apart from the church, the only other part of the priory to survive was the

14th-century gatehouse, on the other side of the River Eea, which now forms an entrance to the village square, from where the walk begins. Take the lane to the left of the post office, past the village hall, through the car park of Cartmel Racecourse and along a track that curves to the left across one corner of the racecourse. Pass through three gates, entering the wooded Lane Park after the third one. Continue through the wood, passing through a gate at the far end and, where the track forks Ⓐ, bear left and head down to a farm, turning left at a junction of paths by the farm Ⓑ and continuing down a track over the river to a road.

Cross over, climb the steps in the wall opposite, at a public footpath sign to Templands via Birkby Hall, and proceed uphill across a field, gradually bearing away from a hedge and wall on the left to climb a ladder-stile. Continue across the next field by a wall on the right, cross a lane and, at a public footpath sign to Allithwaite, keep ahead along a drive that leads up to two large houses; the one on the right is Birkby Hall. Follow footpath directions around the side and back of the house on the left, walk along the edge of the garden and take the path on the right heading uphill through a belt of trees. Climb the

The choir and the great east window of Cartmel Priory

steps ahead and continue across the middle of a field, making for a stile by a gate. Climb it, keep ahead towards farm buildings and climb a stile on the left near a gate separating a hedge from a wall. Continue along the edge of a field to a lane Ⓒ, turn right and, after about 100 yds (91m), turn left along a tarmac track at a public footpath sign to Grange and Lindale.

Keep along this track to another lane, cross over and continue along the edge of a field, squeezing through a narrow gap in a wall ahead and going on to the next lane Ⓓ. Here turn left and then right through a gate, heading uphill across rough pasture. At first keep parallel with the lane on the left but, over the brow, bear right and head in the direction of the right-hand edge of a line of houses in front, making for some steps in the wall ahead. Climb these to rejoin the lane and turn right, following it as it curves left to a crossroads Ⓔ. Here keep ahead along Grange Fell Road and, after passing a golf club on the left, turn left along a narrow uphill lane.

From this lane there are grand views over the Kent estuary and the coastline of Morecambe Bay to the right. By a public footpath sign to Ashmount Road and Charney Road on the right, turn left through a gate onto a path which soon curves to the right and continues as a grassy path stretching ahead, cutting a swathe through the bracken and climbing towards the top of Hampsfield Fell. At a

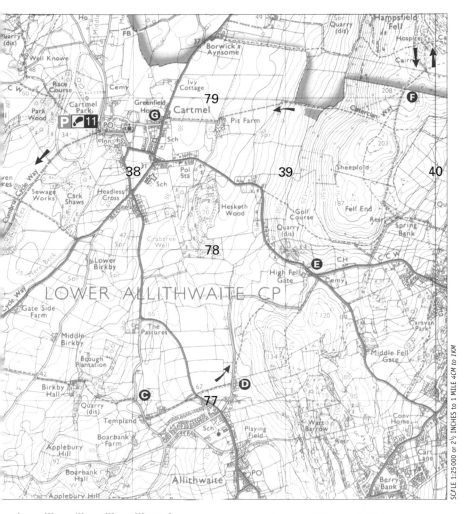

SCALE 1:25000 or 2½ INCHES to 1 MILE 4CM to 1KM

crossing of grassy paths near a telegraph pole **F**, the route turns left to return to Cartmel, but it is well worth while to continue straight ahead for a little over ¼ mile (400m), making for the hospice, a stone hut with an observation platform that marks the summit. For a relatively easy climb and despite being at a modest height (only 727ft/222m), the summit of Hampsfield Fell rewards you with a magnificent panorama that takes in the whole sweep of Morecambe Bay, the Furness peninsula, the Kent estuary, the Pennines and the Lakeland mountains, a view that could hardly be surpassed by any of the much higher and far more challenging fell tops to the north.

Retrace your steps to the crossing of paths near the telegraph pole **F** and turn right, heading downhill and soon getting a glimpse of Cartmel Priory and the village nestling in the valley below. Pass through a metal gate and head across a field, bearing slightly away from a wall on the right, to another gate. Go through, continue across the next field towards farm buildings and, keeping to the right of those buildings, go through a gate in a wall, at a foot-path sign to Cartmel. Carry on across the next field to the road **G**, turn left and immediately right into the village. ●

Wast Water and Irton Fell

Start	Wast Water
Distance	6 miles (9.7km)
Approximate time	4 hours
Parking	Parking-areas by road on western shore of lake
Refreshments	Pubs in Nether Wasdale
Ordnance Survey maps	Landranger 89 (West Cumbria), Outdoor Leisure 6 (The English Lakes – South Western area)

Wast Water, deepest and one of the most remote of the English Lakes, is not friendly; mysterious and brooding, it looks positively menacing and forbidding under dark skies and in misty conditions. The dark screes which drop down to its eastern shores from the heights of Illgill Head only add to this impression. At the same time, however, it has a lonely grandeur and a majestic and awe-inspiring quality which no other lake has, and this walk enables you to appreciate these attributes, both from high above the lake and from its shores. Both the ascent to Irton Fell and the descent from Whin Rigg are steep in parts.

At just under 300ft (91m), Wast Water is England's deepest lake, and among the peaks that preside over it is England's highest mountain, the 3210ft- (978m) high Scafell Pike. The whole area is under the care and protection of the National Trust. Begin by walking along the road by the side of the lake. Opposite are the dark, sheer slopes of the Wast Water screes, which drop over 1700ft (520m) into the lake from Illgill Head. Their instability is the result of glacial action during the Ice Age, which caused the face of Illgill Head to weaken and crumble. Falls still occur.

Turn first left **Ⓐ**, along a road signposted to Gosforth, through a wild, open, rugged landscape. Cross a stream by some houses and, at a public bridleway sign **Ⓑ**, turn immediately left through a gate along a pleasantly

wooded path by a stream. After a while, cross the stream, bear right by a wall on the left, pass through a gate and continue into more open country. Ignoring a stony track which soon swings left, keep ahead along a grassy path, passing two rocky outcrops on the left, making for a gate and ladder-stile. Climb over and keep ahead to go through two more gates. After passing through the second one, turn sharp right, at a public bridleway sign **Ⓒ**, along a path between a wire fence and a line of trees, go through a gate and keep ahead to a T-junction of paths. Here turn left, cross a stream, pass through a gate and keep ahead to another gate. Pass through that and continue ahead, following the direction of the public bridleway sign for Strands, through a farmyard and on to a road.

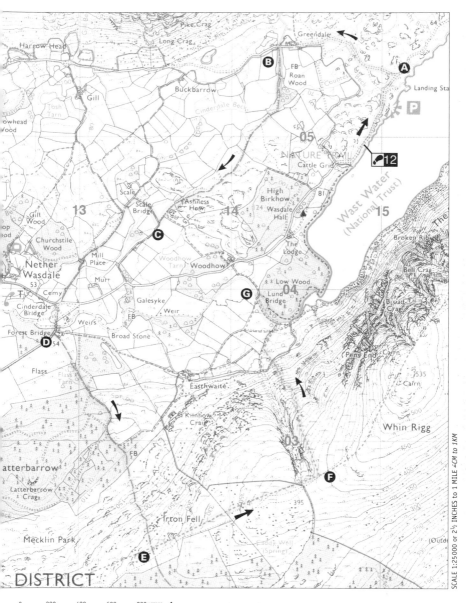

Cross over, take the road signposted to Santon Bridge and Drigg, cross Cinderdale Bridge and, after passing a house, turn left through a gate at a public bridleway sign for Eskdale **D**. Keep ahead towards the trees, climb a stile and, passing to the left of a small tarn, begin the ascent to Irton Fell. Go through a gate and on through plantations, keeping by a wall on the left and continuing to a footpath sign. Here bear left, leaving the wall on the left, through the conifers, over a footbridge and ahead to emerge onto the open fellside. After passing through a double gate, you start to climb more steeply along a clear path that winds up Irton Fell, bearing slightly left past two large boulders.

At the top of the fell and just before more conifer plantations ahead , turn left at a small cairn along a straight path, still climbing, though more gently, and soon picking up a wall on the right. Climb a ladder-stile and continue across the open fell. The path is not clear at this stage, but it keeps climbing in a virtually straight line, eventually levelling off. Go through a broken wall and continue across the top of the steep, rocky ravine of Greathall Gill, bearing left at a small cairn to descend along the right-hand side of the ravine **F**. It is most important to proceed right across the top of the ravine and descend down its right-hand edge. On no account attempt to descend the ravine itself, which soon leads to precipitous drops. As you descend you soon pick up a path that drops steeply towards the foot of the lake. The view ahead, one of the finest in the Lake District, gets better and better as you descend, especially when the classic scene opens up on the right down the length of Wast Water, its

head framed by Great Gable, Kirk Fell, Yewbarrow and Scafell Pike, some of the greatest among English mountains.

Near the bottom, climb a stile, keep ahead to cross a beck on the left and continue down to a stile and gate. Climb over and head across a track into woodland down to the River Irt. Turn left through a gate and keep along the riverbank to Lund Bridge, an attractive old pack-horse bridge **G**. Turn right over it, go through a gate, keep ahead to another gate, pass through that and follow the delightful National Trust path through Low Wood, down to the river again and onto the lakeshore. While enjoying glorious views down the lake towards its head all the way – the classic view seen higher up now enhanced by being framed by trees – follow the lakeshore path through the trees, passing Wasdale Hall on the left, a fine, solid 19th-century mansion, now a youth hostel, in a superb position above Wast Water. Keep ahead to join the road and continue to the parking-area. ●

The classic view towards the head of Wast Water, dominated by Great Gable

Ennerdale Water

Start	Ennerdale Water
Distance	8 miles (12.9km)
Approximate time	4 hours
Parking	Car park by lakeshore
Refreshments	None
Ordnance Survey maps	Landranger 89 (West Cumbria), Outdoor Leisure 4 (The English Lakes – North Western area)

For those who want to stretch their legs and do a reasonably lengthy but easy walk, without climbing, and not too strenuous, this circuit of Ennerdale Water is ideal. Ennerdale Water is the most inaccessible and therefore generally the quietest and least frequented of all the lakes, but its tranquil situation, surrounded by high and rugged fells, gives it a unique grandeur and majesty, appreciated by all who make the effort to visit its lonely shores.

Ennerdale Water had been used as a source of water for the nearby coastal belt for a long time, with a minimal effect on the environment, but in 1980 proposals by the North West Water Authority to raise its level by a further 4ft (1.2m), necessitating the construction of a 10ft (3m) high embankment, met with a storm of protest. The National Park Authority, the local councils, the National Trust, the Countryside Commission and a host of conservationist bodies all combined to oppose them. Unlike earlier attempts to prevent the construction of the Thirlmere and Haweswater reservoirs, this battle was won by the conservationists; not only was the unspoilt beauty of the lake preserved, but this walk, which would have been impossible had the plans been put into effect, also remains.

From the National Trust car park at the foot of the lake, turn left along the lakeshore path. Right from the start, there are glorious views down the length of the lake, with the two closest crags, Bowness Knott and Anglers Crag, on opposite sides of the lake, standing like sentinels at the point where the lake narrows, and, beyond them, the head of the lake, dominated by the 2927ft (892m) high peak of Pillar.

Keep by the lakeshore all the time and follow it round to Bowness Knott. There is a great contrast here between the high and rugged country looking left, towards the head of Ennerdale Water, and the low-lying, softer country looking right, towards the foot of the lake and beyond to the coast.

Continue by the lakeshore in front of the Knott and, about ½ mile (800m) further on, the path joins a tarmac Forestry Commission road, which skirts the edge of conifer plantations. After the land around Ennerdale was purchased by the Forestry Commission and the first dark, thick blanket of conifers, mainly spruce, appeared in the 1920s, the outcry was as great as that

Lonely Ennerdale Water – the most inaccessible of the lakes

the Council for the Preservation of Rural England to leave 300 sq miles (777 sq km) of central Lakeland alone to ensure the preservation of its natural beauty and prevent a repetition of what happened in Ennerdale. With the passage of time, the trees have matured, felling and subsequent restocking have been done more sensitively and with less regimentation, and thus some of the damage to the landscape has been repaired.

aroused by the later Water Board proposals. The result was an agreement in 1936, between the Commission and

This can clearly be seen as you keep along the road past the end of the lake;

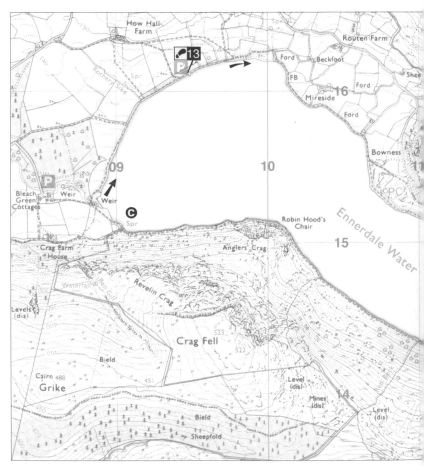

the plantations on the left are edged with silver birches and other hardwoods which, combined with the dramatic view of Pillar in front, makes it a most pleasant walk. Turn right over the first footbridge **Ⓐ** and continue along a well-constructed track, across low-lying meadows near the end of the lake, towards the woods ahead. If this track is flooded, there is an alternative footbridge and parallel path a little way upstream. Just before the woods, turn right, over a ladder-stile **Ⓑ**, walk along the edge of a field, bear left over another stile and continue across meadows towards the end of the lake. Climb a stile and turn right to join the lakeside path.

The path on this side of Ennerdale Water, maintained by the National Trust, is more 'natural': rougher, rockier and altogether more satisfying to walkers. The woodland on this side, clothing the lower slopes of 'The Side', is also more natural and extremely attractive, comprising native hardwoods. It is an easy path, the only difficult section being a bit of rough and steep scrambling over the edge of Anglers Crag, from where the views back towards the head of Ennerdale Water are particularly memorable. At the foot of the lake **Ⓒ** bear right, over a foot-bridge and continue along the lakeshore path, enjoying more grand views, back to the car park.

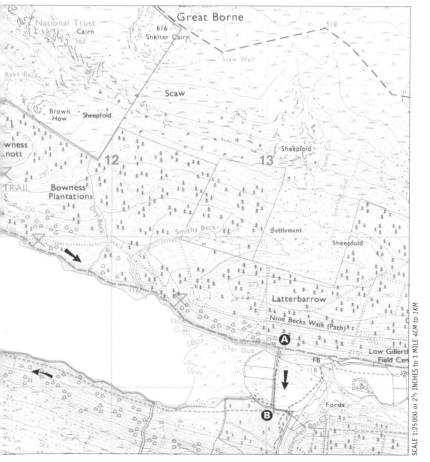

Friar's Crag and Castlerigg Stone Circle

Start	Keswick (lakeshore car park)
Distance	7 miles (11.3km). Shorter version 5½ miles (8.9km)
Approximate time	3½ hours (2½ hours for shorter version)
Parking	Lakeshore car park
Refreshments	Plenty of pubs, restaurants and cafés in Keswick
Ordnance Survey maps	Landranger 90 (Penrith, Keswick & Ambleside), Outdoor Leisure 4 (The English Lakes – North Western area)

Two popular beauty spots, Friar's Crag and Castlehead, as well as a prehistoric stone circle, are featured in this walk, linked by lakeshore, field and woodland paths, which give superb views over Keswick, Derwent Water, Bassenthwaite and the surrounding fells. It makes a most attractive, interesting and varied walk, involving two modest and relatively short climbs, amidst some of the finest scenery the Lake District can offer. It also allows you to combine a good scenic walk with the many delights of nearby Keswick – recreational, cultural and culinary.

Looking around Keswick today, in its magnificent setting between Derwent Water and Bassenthwaite and ringed by fells, it is difficult to imagine it as an industrial town but, from the 16th to the 19th centuries, it was at the centre of an important mining district. The local iron and copper mines suffered from a shortage of skilled labour and, in Elizabeth I's reign, German miners had to be imported into the area. By the late 17th century, most of these mines were worked out but, during the 18th and the early 19th centuries, there was a revival, this time with the mining of graphite (or plumbago), the basis of Keswick's best-known industry, the manufacture of pencils. The last graphite mine closed in 1838, but the pencil and crayon industry

has survived to this day, and among Keswick's unique attractions is a pencil museum. The main street is dominated by the early 19th-century Moot Hall, built on the site of an Elizabethan building. At one time the upper floor was the council chamber and the ground floor a market – now the building is devoted to what is today Keswick's major industry, serving as a tourist information centre. Tourism began in the 19th century with the coming of the railway; although the railway has now gone, the tourists continue to arrive in ever-increasing numbers.

Start by walking along the lakeside road, past the landing-stages for the motor launches and ahead along a wooded track that leads to the end of

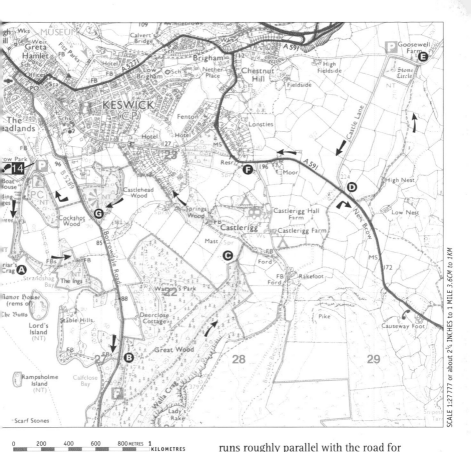

SCALE 1:27777 or about 2¼ INCHES to 1 MILE 3.6CM to 1KM

0 200 400 600 800 METRES 1
KILOMETRES
MILES
0 200 400 600 YARDS ½

Friar's Crag **A**, one of the great scenic high spots of the Lake District. It is not difficult to see why; the views across Derwent Water to Cat Bells and the array of higher peaks behind, and especially the views down the whole length of the lake into the Jaws of Borrowdale, are outstanding.

Turn back from the end of the short promontory and take a path that curves to the right, through a gate and by the lakeshore. Continue over two foot-bridges, turn left through the gate into a wood, keep along a path by the edge of the wood, over another footbridge and bear right to a gate. Pass through, turn left along a broad path up to the Borrowdale road and, just before reaching the road, turn right along a pleasant path through the trees, which runs roughly parallel with the road for ½ mile (800m) to Calfclose Bay. Join the road at a National Trust sign **B**, turn right along it but, after a few yards, cross over to go through a gap in the wall opposite, bearing right through woodland to a car park. Walk straight across the car park to a stile and gate, go through and continue uphill, turning right at a junction of paths. Almost immediately, there is a sharp left turn at a National Trust sign to Walla Crag, along a straight and well-surfaced path that, for the next ½ mile (800m), climbs through the thick conifer woods which clothe the slopes of Walla Crag. Occasional gaps reveal fine vistas over the lake towards Keswick and Skiddaw. The path levels out and descends to a junction of paths. Here take the right-hand fork (signposted Rakefoot and Walla Crag) which briefly climbs again, bearing right to a stile. After climbing this, the woods are left behind and, as you are now in open country and fairly high up, the views for the rest of the way are extensive and mostly unimpeded.

Keep ahead to a little ravine **C**, turn right through a gate and walk along the edge of it, passing through another gate and dropping down to a footbridge. Cross over, head up some steps to a gate, go through and turn left to join the lane ahead. Continue along the lane for a few yards, before turning right at a ladder-stile and gate (public footpath sign to Dale Bottom and Castlerigg Stone Circle) along a grassy path. Keeping along the edge of fields, climb two stiles and, after the second one, turn left along the edge of the next field. Continue over two more ladder-stiles, eventually heading down to a gate and the main Keswick–Windermere road **D**.

If you wish to shorten the walk, you can turn left here along the road, omitting the stone circle.

Otherwise turn right and then first left along a track, passing houses and keeping in a straight line over a succession of stiles, eventually reaching a lane by a wood. Turn left and Castlerigg Stone Circle can be seen in a field on the left **E**. Situated on a plateau and encircled by an impressive series of peaks (Skiddaw, Blencathra, High Dodd, High Rigg, Helvellyn and the Derwent Fells), which form a natural amphitheatre, its setting is certainly dramatic. It comprises thirty-eight stones, grouped in an oval, about 100–110ft (30–34m) in diameter, with a further ten stones outside the circle to the south-east. As is the case with all such circles found in this country, little is known about it. It might date from the neolithic period or the Bronze Age, possibly erected around 1500 BC or earlier. It might have been a religious monument, or a political and administrative centre or a combination of both. It is frustrating not to know

more, but there is no doubt that the mystery only adds to the undeniably powerful atmosphere of the place.

With your back to the entrance gate, climb a stile on the right to gain access to a narrow lane, then turn left and follow it for ¹/₂ mile (800m) back to the main road **D**. Here turn right along this road, which is frequently busy (there is a footpath along one side of it), for another ¹/₂ mile (800m) and, a few yards after passing the sign welcoming you to Keswick, turn left along a lane signposted to Castlerigg and Rakefoot **F**. Past a house on the right there is a public footpath sign. Here turn right through a gate and along a narrow path that bends left and right, proceeds under a footbridge and continues downhill through woodland to Brockle Beck. Cross a footbridge and turn right to follow the beck downhill, through a gate, ahead past a farm, over a bridge and along a tarmac lane.

Keep along this lane past houses for nearly ¹/₂ mile (800m), turning left onto a narrow path at a public footpath sign for Castlehead. Where the path ends, pass through a gate, go up some steps and continue ahead, climbing through thick woodland (there are several paths), eventually to emerge at the top, by a strategically placed seat **G**. Here you can pause to enjoy the finest view of all on a walk of fine views: a magnificent vista of lakes, islands, woodland and rugged peaks, looking across Derwent Water, Keswick and Bassenthwaite.

Descend back through the trees, following the lower slopes of the hill to the left, to pick up a path that leads down, still bearing left, to a gate and steps onto the Borrowdale road. Cross over, go through a gap in the wall opposite, down more steps and along the path straight ahead. On entering woodland once more, turn right, along the edge of the trees, following a path that leads back to the car park. ●

Ravenglass and Muncaster

Start	Ravenglass
Distance	7 miles (11.3km). Shorter version 4½ miles (7.2km)
Approximate time	4 hours (2½ hours for shorter version)
Parking	Ravenglass
Refreshments	Pubs and cafés at Ravenglass, café at Muncaster Castle
Ordnance Survey maps	Landranger 96 (Barrow-in-Furness & South Lakeland), Outdoor Leisure 6 (The English Lakes – South Western area)

Here is a Lakeland walk with a difference: one which begins on the coast. Within its circuit, it includes both a wide range of scenery (seashore, woodland and fell) and varied historic attractions (old port, Roman bath house, castle and 18th-century corn mill). It also enables you to combine the walk with a ride on the major tourist attraction of this remote corner of the national park: the celebrated Ravenglass and Eskdale Railway.

It is hard to believe that this quiet, isolated, one-street village on the edge of the wide, muddy estuary formed by the rivers Irt, Mite and Esk, was once a flourishing port, with a history stretching back to the Roman occupation. The Romans built a fort here (which you pass just after the start of the walk) and it was one of their principal naval bases. In the Middle Ages and later it was an important port for Ireland. Remoteness from major industrial centres and the rise of new ports on the Cumbrian coast caused its decline during the Industrial Revolution but, in the late 19th century, Ravenglass was given a new lease of life when a narrow-gauge railway was built to carry iron ore, passengers and, later, granite from Eskdale down to the coast. The railway was opened in 1875 and survived a number of vicissitudes until its closure in 1960. Then it was

taken over by a preservation society, and the Ravenglass and Eskdale Railway, known affectionately as 'La'al Ratty', now runs regular services from Ravenglass to Dalegarth, using both steam and diesel engines. By the car park is an interesting Railway Museum.

Turn left out of the car park down the main (and indeed the only) street of Ravenglass to where it peters out at the shore, and bear left along the edge of the shore as far as a railway bridge. Turn left under the bridge and bear left along a wide, wooded track to a junction of tracks **Ⓐ**. Here the route turns right but a 100 yds (91m) detour ahead will bring you to the remains of the Roman fort of Glannoventa. Most of the fort, built around AD 130 and abandoned towards the end of the 4th century, has never been excavated and lies under the trees and railway line on

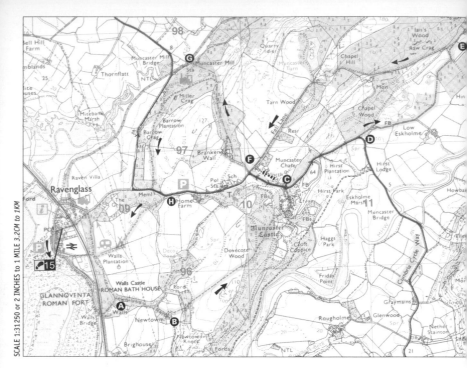

SCALE 1:31250 or 2 INCHES to 1 MILE 3.2CM to 1KM

```
0    200   400   600   800 METRES 1
                                    KILOMETRES
                                    MILES
0    200   400   600 YARDS   ½
```

the other side of the track. The substantial and impressive-looking walls that can be seen, at 12ft (3.5m) high some of the highest-standing walls of any Roman building in the country, are the western end of the bath house, which is detached from the main part of the fort. This was excavated in 1831 and comprises a suite of rooms that would have included changing-rooms and different types of baths (cold, warm and hot).

Retrace your steps to pick up the route and continue along another broad, straight track. Opposite Newtown Cottage, turn left through a gate **B**, at a footpath sign for Muncaster Church and Castle, bear slightly right and walk through a plantation. The first part is rather confusing, but make for the higher ground ahead, soon picking up a discernible path that leads to a stile in a wire fence. Climb over and bear left across open grassland, through a shallow valley between two low hills,

and head uphill in a straight line to a gate in a wall at the edge of a wood. Pass through the gate to follow a most attractive grassy path through Dovecote Wood and into the castle grounds. Soon there is a view of Muncaster Castle through the trees on the right and in a short while you can pay an entrance fee, if you wish, to visit the castle and enjoy its amenities. The path continues downhill, across a play area, by a pond on the left and straight ahead between castle buildings along a tarmac drive. Muncaster Castle has been in the possession of the same family, the Penningtons, since the 13th century and over successive centuries has been enlarged and modernised, to transform the original small 14th-century peel tower into a spacious and comfortable mansion. For giving shelter to Henry VI in 1464, during the Wars of the Roses, Sir John Pennington was presented by the king with the 'Luck of Muncaster', an enamelled glass dish which, as long as it remains unbroken, ensures that the Penningtons will always own

Muncaster. The castle, built in a lovely pink local stone, contains fine tapestries, paintings and furniture. The gardens are renowned for their display of rhododendrons and azaleas in the late spring, and from the castle terrace there is a memorable view up Eskdale.

Passing the tiny Muncaster church on the right, continue to the main road **C**.

*Here walkers who wish to do the shorter alternative can turn left along the road for ¼ mile (400m), rejoining the longer route at **F**.*

Otherwise turn right along the road for ½ mile (800m) but take care; it can be busy and, although it is a main road, it is narrow and has no verge. At a sharp right-hand bend, keep ahead along a clear track **D**, at a public bridleway sign to Muncaster Head and Eskdale and, where that track bears right to a farm, turn left over a stile along another track bordered by trees on the left. All the while, fine views of Eskdale are opening up. Keeping by the edge of the trees, pass through a gate, continue through a conifer plantation, go through another gate and along the right-hand edge of a golf course, turning left across the course at a bridleway sign to a gate. Go through that, turn sharp left **E** along a tarmac track for a few yards and, at a bridleway sign, bear right along a grassy path which climbs steadily through thick conifer woodland. Follow the path to a T-junction, here turning left, at a public bridleway sign for Muncaster, along a wide track called Fell Lane, which leads down to the road. After the long climb through the somewhat gloomy confines of the conifers, it is something of a relief both to get to the top and to emerge into more open country.

At the road, turn right through a gate **F**, at a public bridleway sign, along another broad track which heads up through a farm, before plunging once more into a most attractive wooded valley. Ignore a path to the left and, where there is an open view across the valley of the Mite, keep ahead downhill, soon bearing left towards the river and Muncaster Mill. At a path junction, turn right along a track, and in a few yards turn left down to the mill and railway line **G**. Muncaster Mill is one of the few surviving water-powered corn mills and was the mill serving the manor of Muncaster. The present building dates from the early 18th century, although a mill has been known to exist on this site since the Middle Ages. It closed in 1961 but was restored by the Eskdale (Cumbria) Trust in the late 1970s and is once more in operation, giving a glimpse into a past way of life and enabling visitors to buy a range of freshly milled products.

Retrace your steps to the path junction and, at a bridleway sign for Ravenglass, keep straight ahead along a permissive path. Just past a house on the right, the public footpath is rejoined and you continue ahead, through a gate, keeping parallel with the river below on the right. Go through another gate and keep over the brow of a hill, from where there is a view over the estuary and coast. Pass through a gate, keep ahead a few yards to the road, turn left and, after about 100 yds (91m), turn right along a wooded path at a public footpath sign to Ravenglass **H**. Go through a gate and, with the estuary straight ahead, keep across a large expanse of open grassland (no clear path), gradually bearing left to a metal gate in a wire fence. Pass through, turn right, along the fence, go through another gate and turn right along a tarmac track a few yards ahead. At a public footpath sign 'Railway Station and Ravenglass' turn left through a gate by the side of a house, walk across a children's playground, cross the railway and the car park is straight ahead. ●

Great and Little Langdale

Start	New Dungeon Ghyll Hotel
Distance	8 miles (12.9km)
Approximate time	4 hours
Parking	New Dungeon Ghyll National Park car park – there is also another one 100 yds (91m) further up the road
Refreshments	Old and New Dungeon Ghyll hotels
Ordnance Survey maps	Landranger 90 (Penrith, Keswick & Ambleside), Outdoor Leisure 6 (The English Lakes – South Western area) and 7 (The English Lakes – South Eastern area)

There are two Langdales – Great and Little – separated by Lingmoor Fell. Great Langdale is the more dramatic and rugged, while Little Langdale is less grand and slightly softer, but both valleys are superbly attractive and are popular with walkers. Starting near the head of Great Langdale, framed by the high fells of Crinkle Crags, Bowfell and (inevitably) the Langdale Pikes, the route climbs steeply to the delectable beauty spot of Blea Tarn before dropping down into Little Langdale near the foot of the Wrynose Pass. It continues along to Little Langdale Tarn before climbing back over to Great Langdale for a ramble along the side of the valley to the starting point. This final section is dominated, as indeed is most of the walk, by the twin peaks of Harrison Stickle and Pike of Stickle, better known as the Langdale Pikes, surely the most distinctive and most easily recognisable outline in the whole of the Lake District.

From the car park turn left along the road and, after 100 yds (91m), turn right at a National Trust car park sign for Stickle Gill. Turn immediately left through a gate and cross a field, passing a cottage on the right. Go through a gate, turn right over a footbridge, go through another gate and turn left across another field. The Langdale Pikes tower above on the right and the view ahead is dominated by the bold outlines of Bowfell and Crinkle Crags. Keep by a stream on the left over several stiles and through several gates up to the Old Dungeon Ghyll Hotel. Cross the hotel drive into the next field, turn left through a gate and cross a footbridge to rejoin the road **Ⓐ**.

Keep ahead along the road for a short distance and, where it bends right, bear left over a stile and walk through a camp site, keeping close to a wall on the right and heading towards a belt of trees. Climb two stiles in quick succession, cross a field to a third stile at the edge of a wood, climb over that and keep ahead through the trees to another stile at the far end of the wood.

Climb that and continue, climbing steadily by a wall on the right, over the shoulder of Side Pike, the prominent crag on the left.

At the top, turn right over a ladder-stile onto the road **B**, cross over and, after a few yards, turn left along a path that leads down to Blea Tarn. Pass through a gate into the trees and shrubs that border the tarn, bear slightly left (where the path forks) and, at the end of the tarn, make a few yards' detour to the left, in order to visit one of the most exquisite spots and enjoy one of the loveliest views in the Lake District: the still, quiet waters of Blea Tarn, reflecting trees and fells, backed by the Langdale Pikes; most definitely a place in which to linger. The route continues through a gate and ahead by a stream on the left to drop down into Little Langdale. Later the path bears right, away from the stream, and crosses an area of open grassland and fern to reach the road near the foot of the notorious Wrynose Pass **C**.

Turn left along the road, an important routeway for over 2000 years, used by the Romans to link their forts at Ravenglass, Hardknott and Ambleside via the Hardknott and Wrynose Passes, and later used by pack-horse trains. Keep along it for just over $^1/_2$ mile (800m) and, about 100 yds (91m) past Fell Foot Farm, turn right over a pack-horse bridge **D**, go through a gate and along a walled track ahead. Keep along the track as it curves left along the base of the fell, giving fine views over Little Langdale, the Wrynose Pass, Langdale Pikes and Lingmoor Fell. Soon Little Langdale Tarn, below on the left, is passed and shortly afterwards look out for a stone stile on the left. Climb it and keep ahead to cross a picturesque old pack-horse bridge called Slater Bridge, thought to have been constructed by quarrymen when

The brooding silhouette of the Langdale Pikes

working in the nearby Tilberthwaite Fells. Keep ahead uphill by a wall on the right, going through three gates to reach the road **Ⓔ**.

Turn left and immediately right along a narrow uphill lane, later a rough stony track, which climbs out of Little Langdale and starts to descend once more into Great Langdale. Pass through a gate and, where the track forks, bear left along a path through the trees which drops down, passing quarries on the right, to a tarmac quarry road opposite Crossthwaites Cottage **Ⓕ**. This area is littered with abandoned slate quarries and, ahead in the valley bottom, is the site of an old gunpowder mill which supplied blasting materials to quarries and mines. It only closed in the 1920s and nowadays serves a rather different purpose as a timeshare complex.

Turn left along the quarry road, at first through Baysbrown Wood, and later leaving it to drop down to a farm. Passing the farm on the right, follow what is now a rough track along the

southern slopes of Great Langdale, climbing up into woodland once more and following bridleway signs all the way. Emerging from the trees for the last time, head steadily downhill, bearing right to a barn and turning left in front of the barn along a walled path.

Soon the path drops down to join Great Langdale Beck and the rest of the route is both attractive and relaxing as the path keeps along the side of the valley by the left-hand side of the beck, with the glorious view ahead all the while of the Langdale Pikes and the

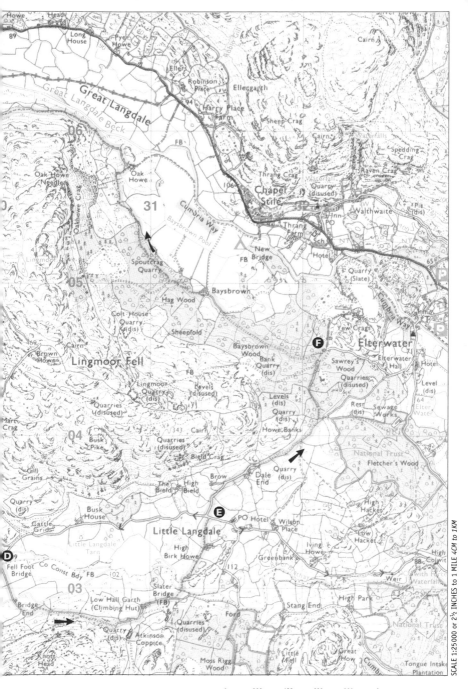

SCALE 1:25000 or 2½ INCHES to 1 MILE 4CM to 1KM

other majestic peaks massed at the head of the dale. Of the two parallel paths at this stage, take the higher one (rather than the one by the beckside) which keeps parallel to a wall on the right, climbs over the beck and finally drops down to Side House Farm. Just before the farm buildings, turn right through a gate and along a drive to the road and car park by the New Dungeon Ghyll Hotel.

●

Cat Bells and Derwent Water

Start	Hawes End, on western side of Derwent Water
Distance	4½ miles (7.2km)
Approximate time	2½ hours
Parking	Small parking-area by roadside. Alternatively go to Hawes End by ferry from Keswick and start the walk from the landing stage
Refreshments	None
Ordnance Survey maps	Landrangers 89 (West Cumbria) and 90 (Penrith, Keswick & Ambleside), Outdoor Leisure 4 (The English Lakes – North Western area)

The ascent of Cat Bells is deservedly one of the most popular walks in the Keswick area – in fact almost too popular, for the National Trust is engaged in a constant battle against footpath erosion on both the main routes to the top. Despite its modest height (1481ft/451m), both ascent and descent, though short, are quite steep and strenuous, and the Cat Bells ridge walk is one of the finest, offering glorious panoramas across Derwent Water and down Borrowdale to the left and over the Newlands valley to the right. A delightful stroll along the wooded shores of Derwent Water rounds off a superb walk.

From the small, roadside parking-area by a cattle-grid, go through a gate and

The peaks of Cat Bells and Causey Pike rise above Derwent Water

bear right at a footpath sign for Cat Bells. Following National Trust signs, take the steep zigzag path up the slopes, and immediately you start to enjoy the grand views over Derwent Water. The path is well marked and initially disgorges you at a preliminary summit. Ahead, standing out prominently and invitingly, is the main summit of Cat Bells. Drop down to a small col and then continue ahead, climbing steeply up a rough path to the top **Ⓐ**, from where there unfolds one of the finest of Lakeland vistas: a magnificent view to the left over Keswick and Derwent Water, backed by the wooded slopes of Walla Crag and Castlehead, with Blencathra looming on the horizon; in front, looking towards the Jaws of Borrowdale; to the right, over the Newlands valley and fells and behind, over Bassenthwaite Lake and the brooding mass of Skiddaw. Incidentally, Cat Bells gets its name from the wildcats which used to roam throughout the Lake District, until the end of the 18th century, by which time they had more or less died out.

Keep ahead, starting to descend from the summit, and drop down into the next col **B**. Here turn left along a path that zigzags steeply downhill, eventually straightening out and heading diagonally towards the far end of the trees below. Keep along this path as it curves round the edge of the wood to a gate, go through and bear right, down to a road **C**.

Turn sharp left along the road and, at a National Trust sign near a small parking-area, bear right through a gate **D**, along a broad, well-surfaced track through Manesty Woods. Keep ahead, following footpath signs to Brandelhow and Hawes End, to reach the lakeshore at Abbot's Bay, by a boathouse. Pass through two gates in fairly quick succession and then follow a delightful wooded path through Brandlehow Park by the shores of Derwent Water for 1¼ miles (2km), with fine views across the lake all the while. At one stage, partially hidden by vegetation, are the spoil-heaps of a lead and silver mine, evidence that in past centuries this was an important mining area. These woods were one of the first acquisitions made by the recently formed National Trust in 1902.

Go through a gate by the Hawes End landing stage and turn left by the edge

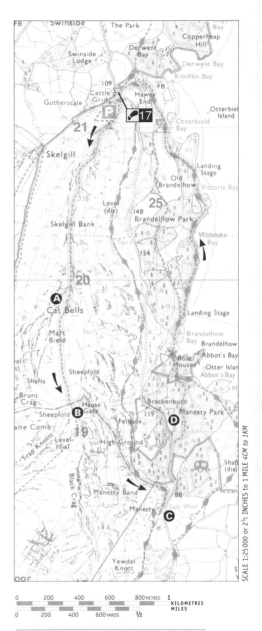

SCALE 1:25 000 or 2½ INCHES to 1 MILE 4CM to 1KM

of a wall, from where there is an excellent view of Cat Bells. Follow the path through a kissing-gate, keep ahead to another kissing-gate, go through that and bear right along a tarmac track. Just past Hawes End House, turn left away from the track along a wooded path which, in a few yards, comes out onto the road by the parking-area. ●

Sawrey and Claife Heights

Start	Ash Landing car park, on western shore of Windermere near the car ferry point for Bowness
Distance	6½ miles (10.5km)
Approximate time	3½ hours
Parking	Ash Landing car park. Alternatively use one of the car parks on the eastern side of the lake and come across on the ferry
Refreshments	Pub and tearooms in Near Sawrey
Ordnance Survey maps	Landranger 96 (Barrow-in-Furness & South Lakeland), Outdoor Leisure 7 (The English Lakes – South Eastern area)

Between Esthwaite Water and the western shores of Windermere lie the thickly wooded Claife Heights, which are steep-sided on their eastern side. The entire area provides a varied mixture of pleasant, shady forest walks, with intermittent forays into more craggy, open country, from which there are splendid views up and down Windermere. Nearby is the village of Near Sawrey, famous as the home of Beatrix Potter. Some difficult conditions underfoot can be expected in places on the forest paths, with tree roots and rocks to negotiate and some muddy sections.

Turn right out of the car park and walk along the road to Hawkshead for ¾ mile (1.2km). Just past Hawkrigg Farm, turn left, at a public footpath sign **A**, along a narrow path that squeezes between a fence on the left and a wall on the right. Go through a gate and, with fine views of rolling, wooded hills ahead, keep along the edge of a field, through a gate in the wall on the right and across to another gate near St Peter's Church, the parish church serving both Far and Near Sawrey.

Go through this gate, keep ahead to a lane and turn right **B**. The village of Far Sawrey is just ahead. Walk past the cluster of cottages at Town End, turn left through a gate at a public footpath sign and keep straight ahead across

meadows to a footbridge. Cross it, bear right by the side of a stream, cross another footbridge and go through a gate to rejoin the road, turning left into Near Sawrey.

Beatrix Potter's house, Hill Top, is on the left as you enter the village. It was partly from the royalties of *The Tale of Peter Rabbit* that Beatrix Potter was able to buy the 17th-century farmhouse of Hill Top, which became her home for the rest of her life. Most of her perennially popular children's stories were written here and set in the surrounding area. The house is now a Beatrix Potter Museum and many of her original drawings are on display there.

In the village centre, turn right along a lane **C**, between cottages and past a

SCALE 1:25000 or 2½ INCHES to 1 MILE 4CM to 1KM

| 0 | 200 | 400 | 600 | 800 METRES | 1 KILOMETRES |
| 0 | 200 | 400 | 600 YARDS | ½ | MILES |

farm, continuing along a wide, walled track at a public bridleway sign. The track climbs steadily, giving fine views over a perhaps uncharacteristically gentle, green, wooded landscape. Keep ahead, climbing all the while along the main track (walled both sides most of the time) to Moss Eccles Tarn, a pleasant spot enfolded by sloping meadows and woods. Just past the tarn at a junction

of paths, keep straight ahead, still climbing gently and soon passing the right-hand edge of Wise Een Tarn, with a shallow fishpond on the right. As you climb, you will see more typical Lakeland views over the higher fells beyond the tarn, including the Langdale Pikes.

Following bridleway signs, head up to a gate and stile to enter woodland. The path passes a small, reedy tarn surrounded by trees on the right and keeps ahead, now with fine views over

Hill Top, Near Sawrey – Beatrix Potter's home

in 1781. She and her husband not only landscaped the grounds of their house and the island but also planted much of the lovely woodland on the western shores of the lake, through which you soon walk, a pleasant change and a striking contrast with the conifers.

Continue down and then up to a footpath sign by a large rock. Turn left by the side of the rock and take the path that drops down and up again to another open, rocky clearing with more fine views, this time towards the lower end of Windermere. Turn left at a public footpath sign to Ferry and head down through the trees once more, turning right at another footpath sign. The path continues straight ahead, but a few yards' detour to the left out of the trees brings you to a headland overlooking the lake for the best view of all; a marvellous place for photographs and picnics **F**.

Return to the path which soon bears right and winds downhill through an area of more mixed woodland and open country. Climb a stile and keep along a broad path, by a wall on the left, passing through a gate to leave the woods and continuing down to a junction of paths **G**. Here turn left along another broad path, signposted to Belle Grange, skirting woodland on the right, and at a footpath sign to Ferry turn right through a gate. At first head through the middle of the woods, later following a path across fields, with Windermere visible through the trees below on the left. Finally descend steeply through Station Scar Wood, passing by a ruined building, back to the car park. ●

Latterbarrow and the fells at the head of Windermere. Where the track follows a sharp left-hand bend, turn right, at a public footpath sign to Ferry, onto a narrow path through thick conifers **D**. It is fortunate that the remainder of the route, mostly through dense woodland with occasional clearings, is well-waymarked, because otherwise it would be both confusing and difficult to follow and tedious to describe in detail. Simply look out for the regular white waymarks and you cannot go wrong.

At a small clearing, turn right through more thick conifer woodland along an undulating path that passes the viewpoint over Windermere shown on the map and finally descends to a broad stony track. Here turn right for a few yards and, at a footpath sign for Ferry, bear left off the track, once more plunging into dense woodland. The path keeps straight for a while, then turns sharp right uphill at white waymarks, where a few yards' detour to the left will soon bring you to a magnificent view over Windermere and Belle Isle, with the houses of Bowness directly opposite **E**. On Belle Isle is an unusual circular house, built by a Mr English in 1774 and purchased by Mrs Isabella Curwen of Workington Hall

Crummock Water, Mosedale and Rannerdale

Start	Buttermere
Distance	9½ miles (15.3km)
Approximate time	5 hours
Parking	Buttermere
Refreshments	Pubs in Buttermere, pub at Loweswater
Ordnance Survey maps	Landranger 89 (West Cumbria), Outdoor Leisure 4 (The English Lakes – North Western area)

Crummock Water is bounded by the towering peaks of Mellbreak and Grasmoor, which rise up steeply and abruptly from the lakeshore. The two quiet lonely valleys on either side of it are less frequented than many others in the Lake District, and this walk explores both of them in the course of an enlarged circuit of the lake. It also takes in a popular waterfall and, towards the end, provides a dramatic, bird's-eye view over both Crummock Water and Buttermere. It is a reasonably lengthy walk but there are only two climbs on it, both of which are modest ones.

Start by taking the path to the left of the Fish Hotel, follow it around to the left, through a gate and, where the main path bears right, turn sharp right through another gate at a footpath sign to Scale Bridge and Scale Force. Follow a path down to Scale Bridge **Ⓐ**, cross over, turn right and head towards Crummock Water, dominated by the peaks of Mellbreak on the left and Grasmoor on the right, following the stream on the right. On approaching the lake, the path bears left and climbs above it, giving most striking views down its length. Continue bearing left all the while along the cairned path that follows the edge of the valley, keeping to the higher, and therefore drier, level. On reaching Scale Beck, keep by it in order to see Scale Force, the highest waterfall in the Lake District, where the

water plunges over 170ft (52m) in a single drop **Ⓑ**.

Cross the footbridge on the right and turn right along the other bank of the beck, heading downhill. Look out for a footbridge on the left, cross it, climb a stile a few yards ahead and bear left up the slope. Bear left again to join a path that follows the right-hand edge of the valley, part of an ancient route between Buttermere and Ennerdale. Climb towards the head of the valley and, just before reaching a stile in front, turn right **Ⓒ**, keep by the fence on the left to a stile, climb over and follow a grassy path ahead through Mosedale. This lonely and austere valley, hemmed in by the Loweswater Fells on the left and Mellbreak on the right, is virtually treeless, apart from the isolated Mosedale Holly Tree, marked on the Ordnance Survey map

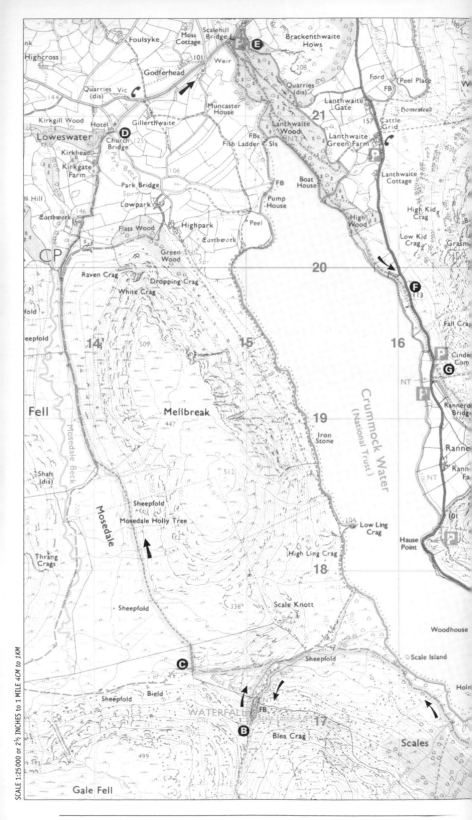

SCALE 1:25000 or 2½ INCHES to 1 MILE 4CM to 1KM

and soon conspicuous on the left. Keep along this path for $2\frac{1}{2}$ miles (4km); at first it is narrow, but it later broadens out into a track. Near a plantation, Loweswater can be seen over to the left.

Eventually go through a gate, along a walled track, over Church Bridge and ahead to the small, 19th-century Loweswater church **D**. Here turn right (on the left is the Kirkstile Inn), right again at a T-junction and keep along a lane for $\frac{1}{2}$ mile (800m) to Scalehill Bridge. Just after crossing the bridge over the River Cocker, turn right at a public bridleway sign **E** into Langthwaite Wood, go through a gate a few yards ahead and keep along a broad track, parallel to the river on the right. Stay on the main track all the time down to the lakeshore,

Crummock Water overshadowed by Whiteless Pike

from where there is a marvellous view down the length of Crummock Water looking towards Buttermere.

Turn left and follow a path through trees and along the edge of the lake, climbing over several stiles, eventually to come out onto the road **F**. Turn right along the road, walk through a small car park and bear left **G** over a beck and across open country to enter the narrow valley of Rannerdale. Keep parallel with a wall on the right, soon picking up a broad grassy path. Climb a stile, continue heading up the dale, cross a footbridge on the right, climb a ladder-stile ahead and turn left, following a wall on the left. This is a most pleasant, quiet and attractive part of the walk, as the path recrosses the beck and continues to the head of the dale.

At a path junction **H**, turn right and take the path that winds downhill, across bracken and by rocks, giving the finest view of the walk: a dramatic vista over both Buttermere and Crummock Water, backed by some of the most rugged mountain terrain in the country. Head towards Buttermere village below, bearing left to a wall. Look out for a gate and stile in that wall, climb over, turn right and follow the path along the edge of the little ravine of Ghyll Wood, which drops straight down into Buttermere. ●

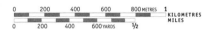

Wansfell and Troutbeck

Start	Ambleside
Distance	6½ miles (10.5km)
Approximate time	4 hours
Parking	Ambleside
Refreshments	Plenty of pubs, cafés and restaurants in Ambleside, pub at Troutbeck
Ordnance Survey maps	Landranger 90 (Penrith, Keswick & Ambleside), Outdoor Leisure 7 (The English Lakes – South Eastern area)

This splendid walk comprises a high-level outward route from Ambleside to Troutbeck over the summit of Wansfell (1588ft/484m), followed by a lower-level return route, the latter part of which passes through the delightful Skelghyll Wood. From both levels the views over the surrounding fells and down the length of Windermere, England's longest lake, are magnificent. Despite its modest height, the ascent of Wansfell is quite long and tiring but the descent into the Troutbeck valley is relatively easy, as is the remainder of the walk.

Situated on a main road at the head of Windermere, Ambleside has developed into one of the Lake District's major tourist centres. Although a visitor might come away with the overriding impression of a 19th-century town, the period when most of its hotels and guest houses were built, Ambleside is not just a creation of the Victorian tourist era; the Romans built their fort of Galava here, an important centre for their communications network in north-west England. At the far end of the town stands what is undoubtedly Ambleside's most photographed building: the tiny 17th-century Bridge House, built above the bridge over Stock Ghyll and now a National Trust information centre.

Start at Bridge House and walk along the road in the direction of Windermere to the town centre. Where the road bends right, keep ahead, between the Market Hall and Barclays Bank, following signs to 'The Waterfalls'. In a while, the road joins Stock Ghyll on the left and follows the beck up its wooded valley. Bear left along a path which leads up to Stockghyll Force, a series of falls which look most impressive as they cascade down the wooded ravine. Walk up by the side of the falls and, just before the top, turn sharp right at a T-junction along a broad path, then pass through a turnstile and keep ahead to a public footpath sign for Kirkstone.

Here turn left along a tarmac track, go through a gate and continue ahead, still parallel with the beck below. In a short while, turn right and climb two stiles, at a footpath sign to Troutbeck via Wansfell **A**. Now a steady ascent

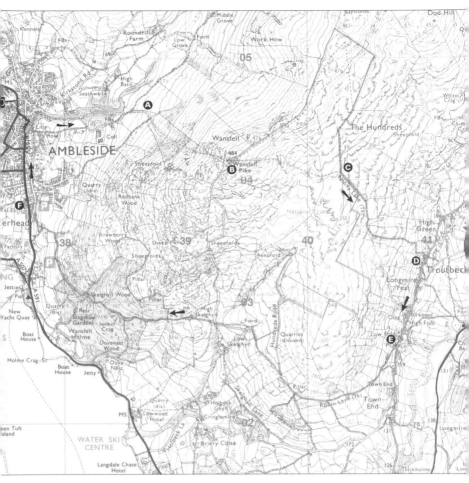

```
0    200   400   600  800 METRES 1
                               KILOMETRES
                               MILES
0    200   400   600 YARDS  ½
```

begins, fairly gentle at first but later
quite steep, along a path that keeps by a
beck on the left. The higher you climb
the more outstanding the views become,
with Ambleside down in the valley
below, surrounded by wooded slopes
and backed by an array of dramatic
peaks, looking like an Alpine resort.
Past the top of the treeline the path
crosses the beck, and the route ahead is
now marked by cairns. It is quite hard
going but the reward is a magnificent
view over much of southern and central
Lakeland, including the Coniston,
Langdale, Sca Fell and High Street Fells,

almost the whole length of Windermere
and, beyond, Morecambe Bay, Furness
and the Pennines.

Near the actual summit of Wansfell
Pike **B**, which is a short detour to the
left, climb a ladder-stile and keep
ahead, following a line of cairns, to
start dropping down into the Troutbeck
valley. Go through a gate, keep ahead to
another gate, go through that, turn right
C along a walled track called Nanny
Lane and follow it into Troutbeck. At
the road **D** turn right through the
village, which is old and distinctive-
looking, strung out with green slate and
whitewashed farms and cottages, many
of which date back to the 17th and 18th
centuries. At the southern end of the

village is the National Trust property of Town End, a particularly fine example of a 17th-century yeoman farmer's house, containing much of its original furniture and utensils.

Just past the post office on the right, bear right at a public bridleway sign for Ambleside Ⓔ along an uphill walled track, called Robin Lane. Where it starts to level out, fine views over Windermere begin to open up again. At another public bridleway sign for Ambleside, turn left off the track, pass through a gate and keep ahead along a broad path. Continue through a gate by a stream, turn right, along a tarmac road, go past a farm, through a gate and keep straight ahead, shortly entering Skelghyll Wood. The path now winds through this most attractive wood to the celebrated viewpoint of Jenkin Crag, a short detour to the left at a National Trust sign. From this rocky spur above the trees, there is a spectacular view down Windermere, one of the highlights of the walk.

Return to the path and continue through the wood, soon starting to drop down towards Ambleside. There are several paths but keep along the main one, roughly parallel with the road below, eventually turning left down a walled lane and past houses to that same road Ⓕ. Here turn right, back into the town centre of Ambleside. ●

Looking down Windermere from Jenkin Crag

Buttermere and Hay Stacks

Start	Buttermere
Distance	7½ miles (12.1km). Buttermere only 4½ miles (7.2km)
Approximate time	5 hours (2½ hours for shorter alternative)
Parking	Buttermere
Refreshments	Pubs in Buttermere
Ordnance Survey maps	Landrangers 89 (West Cumbria) and 90 (Penrith, Keswick & Ambleside), Outdoor Leisure 4 (The English Lakes – North Western area)

Whether viewed from its shores or from the heights surrounding it, Buttermere is regarded as one of the most beautiful of the smaller lakes. This walk, which combines a circuit of the lake with an ascent of Hay Stacks, enables you to sample both types of view as well as climbing one of the best-loved Lakeland peaks. The climb is steep and tiring, but take your time, pause frequently to admire the scenery and you will enjoy a walk of immense beauty and variety. For those who simply want a short and easy walk, or if the weather is unsuitable for climbing Hay Stacks, a circuit of the lake alone makes an excellent alternative.

The small village of Buttermere lies between Buttermere and Crummock Water amidst some of the grandest Lakeland scenery. At one time the two lakes were one, but as debris deposited by streams gradually built up, the alluvial plain on which the village stands was formed. The village itself consists of little apart from two hotels, a few farms and houses and a small, plain 19th-century church standing on a rocky ledge above the village, but it is an excellent walking centre, offering both gentle lakeside strolls and tough mountain hikes or, as in this case, a combination of both.

From the car park walk back up to the road and turn right. After a few yards, turn right again, at a public bridleway sign saying 'Lakeshore Path', and keep ahead, soon approaching the lake. From the very beginning, the views across Buttermere to the array of peaks beyond: Red Pike, High Stile, High Crag, Hay Stacks and Fleetwith Pike, are most impressive. Do not go through the gate ahead, but turn right down to the lakeshore, go through a gate and bear left to follow a most attractive path along the edge of the lake. Keep along it for about a mile (1.6km), through several gates and, at one point, under a tunnel, eventually bearing left to rejoin the road **A**. Turn right along the road to Gatesgarth Farm.

At this point, walkers who simply wish to do the circuit of the lake can turn right and follow a path across the end of the lake, rejoining the longer route at **E**.

Continue over Gatesgarthdale Beck, and, just past a cottage on the right, turn right at a bridleway sign onto a stony path **B**. This path winds around to enter the valley of Warnscale Bottom, surrounded by towering fells with Hay Stacks on the right. Bear right, away from the main path and over a footbridge to start the tough part of the walk: a steep and unremitting climb by the side of Warnscale Beck up to the top of Green Crag. The superb views over Buttermere behind are a good excuse for several rests, the last stretch being particularly steep and rocky. Bear right, to continue between two sets of crags and, at the top, bear right again. The path is easy to follow.

Now the steepest part of the walk is over. Keep along this path, lined with cairns and with dramatic views and sheer drops to the right, through a wilderness of crags, peaks and boulders, past Blackbeck Tarn, ahead via the exquisite Innominate Tarn and finally to the summit of Hay Stacks, where there is also a small tarn. From this height, (it is just over 1900ft (579m) and

Looking across Buttermere to the distinctive outline of Hay Stacks

so, being under the magic figure of 2000ft (610m) it is not, technically speaking, a mountain, although it certainly looks and feels like one), there are extensive views down Ennerdale, its lower slopes thickly forested, and Buttermere, and among the prominent peaks that can be seen are High Crag, Pillar, Kirk Fell, Great Gable and the Newland Fells.

Keep ahead at the summit, dropping down steeply into the col between Hay Stacks and High Crag. Here turn right **C** to pick up the path through Scarth Gap Pass, a route over the fells between Buttermere and Ennerdale, which soon starts dropping down towards Buttermere, giving more superb views. Approaching the lake, keep straight ahead at a path junction,

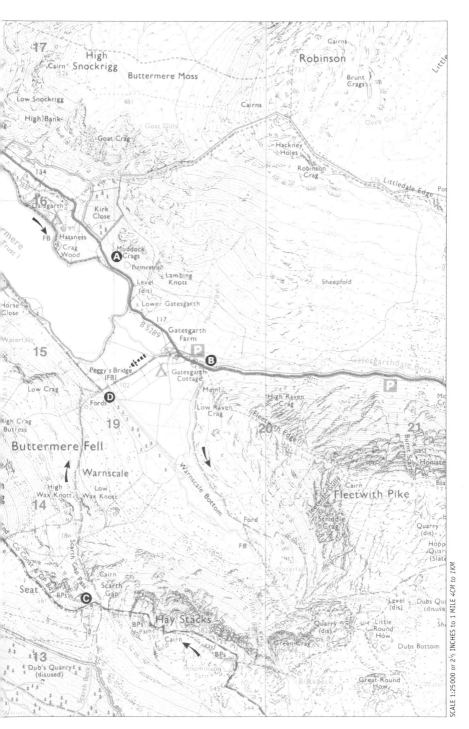

SCALE 1:25000 or 2½ INCHES to 1 MILE 4CM to 1KM

continue down to a wall and bear left **D**, following the edge of the lake. Keep along this lakeshore path, which is maintained by the National Trust, through Burtness Wood for 1¼ miles (2km). At the end of the lake, turn right **E**, go through a gate, keep ahead over a footbridge, bear right across another bridge and follow the path back to the starting point in Buttermere. ●

Ashness Bridge, Watendlath and Bowder Stone

Start	Kettlewell car park on the eastern shore of Derwent Water
Distance	8½ miles (13.7km)
Approximate time	5 hours
Parking	Kettlewell car park by the lakeshore. Alternatively, use Watendlath road car park, where the road to Watendlath branches off the Borrowdale road, and start the walk from there
Refreshments	Cafés at Watendlath and Grange
Ordnance Survey maps	Landrangers 89 (West Cumbria) and 90 (Penrith, Keswick & Ambleside), Outdoor Leisure 4 (The English Lakes – North Western area)

This is an exceptionally beautiful walk, which has three scenic highlights that will remain indelibly in the memory. The first is the well-known viewpoint from Ashness Bridge over Derwent Water and Skiddaw. Next, from a wooded perch high above the valley, comes the dramatic Surprise View. Finally, there is the magnificent view of the head of Borrowdale soon after leaving Watendlath. Lakeshore, woodland, a huge isolated boulder and an idyllic secluded hamlet make this an outstandingly varied walk. The terrain is good throughout and there are only two modest climbs.

Start by turning right along the lake-shore and follow the curve of the shore around to rejoin the road by the Ashness landing-stage **A**. Go up some steps and take the narrow uphill lane straight ahead, which is signposted to Ashness Bridge and Watendlath. Climb to the old pack-horse bridge and look back to enjoy the magnificent panorama, a classic view which is a forerunner for the even more magnificent Surprise View, about ½ mile (800m) further along the lane.

Surprise View is a precarious ledge on the edge of woodland, with a steep drop below, from where the view over Borrowdale, Derwent Water, Keswick and Bassenthwaite, with Skiddaw forming the dramatic backcloth, must surely be one of the most outstanding in the country. From here follow a delightful path through the woods parallel to the lane. At a wall climb a ladder-stile, turn right over Watendlath Beck **B** and turn left to follow the beck, initially through woodland and later across meadows and below crags, for

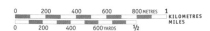

0	200	400	600	800 METRES	1
					KILOMETRES
					MILES
0	200	400	600 YARDS	½	

1 1/2 miles (2.4km) into the idyllic, isolated hamlet of Watendlath. This is a lovely spot on the shores of Watendlath Tarn, nothing more than a small collection of farmhouses, but noted as the setting for the home of Judith Paris in the novels of Sir Hugh Walpole (1884–1941).

At Watendlath go through a gate **C**, bear right along the edge of the tarn, pass through another gate and, at a fork, keep ahead along the uphill path at a public bridleway sign for Rosthwaite. The path climbs steadily, providing grand views behind over Watendlath. Where it levels off and starts to drop down into Borrowdale, there are magnificent views ahead of the white cottages of Rosthwaite, the lush green meadows below in the valley and the woods on the lower slopes of the fells; looking towards Honister, the head of the dale can be seen, framed by majestic and awe-inspiring peaks.

Descend by trees on the right, turn right through a gate, at a footpath sign for Keswick and Bowder Stone **D**, and take a path that drops down to a gate, then passes into woods and continues to a road. Turn right along the road for

The secluded hamlet of Watendlath

1/4 mile (400m) and by a gate turn right over a stile at a National Trust sign to Bowder Stone **E**. Follow a broad wooded path to the stone, an immense, isolated boulder left by retreating glaciers during the last Ice Age. It is estimated to weigh over 2000 tons and a ladder on one side enables closer inspection and the opportunity to take in the view from the top.

Continue ahead to rejoin the Borrow-dale road and keep along it, with good views of High Spy and Maiden Moor on the left, turning left over the old narrow bridge across the Derwent **F** into Grange.

Walk through the village and along the lane for nearly 3/4 mile (1.2km), turning right through a gate at a public footpath sign to Lodore **G**. The path crosses low-lying, marshy grazing land, with convenient boardwalks in places, skirting Manesty Woods and bearing right across the foot of Derwent Water, with excellent views down the lake. Continue over the river and ahead to the Borrowdale road again **H**. Turn left along the road back to the car park; just past the Lodore Swiss Hotel you can walk along a pleasant National Trust path running parallel to the road through Strutta Wood, rejoining the road opposite the car park. ●

Haweswater, High Street and Harter Fell

Start	Haweswater
Distance	7 miles (11.3km)
Approximate time	4½ hours
Parking	Car park at Mardale Head at southern end of lake
Refreshments	None
Ordnance Survey maps	Landranger 90 (Penrith, Keswick & Ambleside), Outdoor Leisure 5 (The English Lakes – North Eastern area)

Haweswater is not a natural lake but a large reservoir, which inevitably gives it an artificial appearance, particularly at close quarters. Despite this, its head is encircled by high fells, which offer plenty of good, scenic and challenging walks, such as this one. The route climbs steeply and steadily from the head of the lake, along the edge of Riggindale, to the flat grassy summit of High Street. From here a splendid ridge walk continues to the neighbouring summits of Mardale III Bell and Harter Fell before dropping down, via the Gatescarth Pass, back to the lake. This is preferably a fine weather walk with good clear paths and outstanding views.

Before the construction of the reservoir, the wooded, fertile valley of Mardale had only a small lake in it and farms, a village and a church. In 1940, however, Manchester Corporation built a dam across the foot of the lake, raising its water level by nearly 100ft (30m), and the village, farms and valley were submerged. Hence Haweswater arose, and since then it has attracted both praise and criticism; criticism for the destruction of a community and the despoiling of a beautiful valley, and praise for what is an impressive expanse of water, especially when seen from the high fells massed at its head. In the exceptionally dry summer of 1984, the water level dropped so low

that the ruins of the village of Mardale were visible once more; a somewhat eerie sight. One factor common to both the pre- and post-reservoir eras is the comparative inaccessibility of the area; it can be reached only by one narrow cul-de-sac lane that runs along the eastern side of the lake, terminating at the Mardale Head car park.

Turn right out of the car park, go through a gate and keep ahead to a junction of three paths by a footpath sign. Take the path on the right, which curves around the head of the lake Ⓐ and continues along the edge of a plantation on the right. Just before reaching a wall in front, turn sharp left Ⓑ (almost doubling back on your tracks) along a path which climbs steeply towards the crags ahead, giving the most spectacular views looking down the length of Haweswater; views that could hardly be surpassed at any of the natural lakes. The path continues along a ridge high above Riggindale on the right and Mardale on the left, past a whole series of crags. After negotiating Rough Crag, a splendid ridge walk along Long Stile stretches ahead, looking like another Striding Edge and climbing towards the summit of High Street. To the left, across the dark tarn of lovely Blea Water, the rocky slopes of Harter Fell stand out clearly, while over to the right, across the uninhabited bare expanses of Riggindale, Kidsty Pike can be seen.

At the top ⓒ, bear left across a surprisingly smooth grassy plateau, heading towards the triangulation pillar which marks the summit of High Street, at 2719ft (828m) one of the major Lakeland peaks, despite its smooth appearance and relatively easy ascent. A Roman road ran along the top of High Street, linking the forts at Ambleside and Brougham, the highest Roman road in the country. It is still

Dramatic fells frame the head of Haweswater

used today as a footpath, running straight and true across the top. The flat top of High Street has been used for other purposes: horse-racing, wrestling

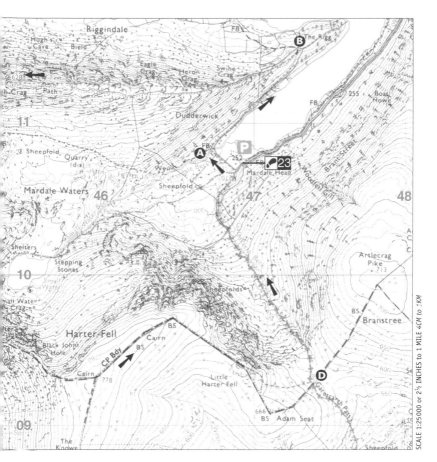

contests, drinking, feasting and dancing for the people living in the nearby dales; hence the alternative name of Racecourse Hill. From here, there is one of the finest all-round views in the area, taking in Morecambe Bay, the Coniston range, the Langdale Pikes, Helvellyn, Place Fell and the line of the Pennines.

Walk along the flat surface of the summit, by a wall on the right, and soon a grand view down the whole length of Windermere unfolds. In a short while, turn left to pick up a path which crosses the cliffs above the head of Mardale, descending slightly and then climbing gently to the summit of Mardale III Bell (2496ft/761m), from where there is another grand view, looking down past the aptly named tarn of Small Water to the curving length of

Haweswater beyond. Keep ahead to descend to the Nan Bield Pass, a pack-horse route between Mardale and the Kentmere valley, and continue straight ahead, climbing quite steeply to the third summit on the route, Harter Fell (2539ft/778m).

Keep past the summit cairn, topped with iron fence posts which give it a decidedly weird shape, by a fence on the right, to drop down to the Gatescarth Pass, another old pack-horse route, this time between Mardale and Longsleddale **D**. Here turn sharp left and follow a path that winds downhill by Gatescarth Beck back to the car park at Mardale Head.   ●

Birks Bridge, Hardknott and Harter Fell

Start	Birks Bridge
Distance	7 miles (11.3km)
Approximate time	4 hours
Parking	Forestry Commission's Dunnerdale Forest car park just above Birks Bridge
Refreshments	None
Ordnance Survey maps	Landrangers 89 (West Cumbria), 90 (Penrith, Keswick & Ambleside) and 96 (Barrow-in-Furness & South Lakeland), Outdoor Leisure 6 (The English Lakes – South Western area)

A magnificent scenic walk around Harter Fell (a different Harter Fell from the one climbed on the last walk). This one rises 2140ft (653m) above the rugged terrain of Eskdale and Dunnerdale, two of the wildest, loveliest and loneliest Lakeland valleys. The route starts along the banks of the Duddon and then climbs out of the valley to the remains of Hardknott Roman fort, perched high above Upper Eskdale. It continues over the lower slopes of Harter Fell, before ascending steeply to the summit and finally dropping down, equally steeply on loose ground through plantations back into the Duddon valley. There are some lengthy and steep sections of climbing across rough country to be encountered.

The Duddon was Wordsworth's favourite river, so much so that he wrote thirty-five sonnets in praise of it, and much of this walk shows why. Even the recent plantations in Dunnerdale Forest have done little to impair its unrivalled beauty.

At the car park, cross the bridge over the Duddon and turn right along a riverside path. Climb a stile and continue by the sparkling river, amidst glorious scenery, for 1 mile (1.6km), before bearing left towards Black Hall Farm. Just before reaching the farm buildings, turn sharp left through a gate Ⓐ, cross a field towards a group of rocks, pass through a gap in a wall and turn left. Keep along the side of the wall for about 100 yds (91m) before bearing right, uphill over rough grassland towards the edge of the conifer plantations. There is no clear path at this stage, but head towards the trees, keeping just to the right of the plantation boundary wall. Climb a ladder-stile in a wall in front and continue steeply upwards, veering slightly right after arriving at the top of the ridge and passing the end of the trees.

At the top, a magnificent view down the whole length of Eskdale unfolds, with the playing-card outline of the

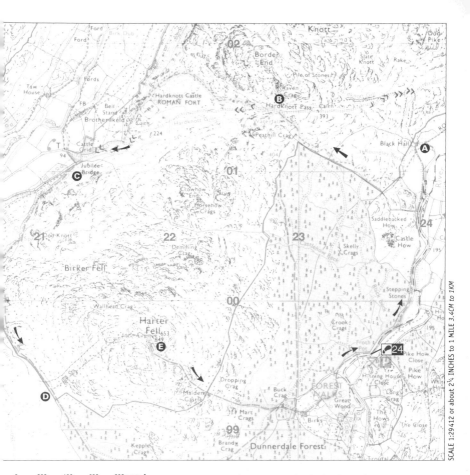

SCALE 1:29412 or about 2¼ INCHES to 1 MILE 3.4CM to 1KM

| 0 | 200 | 400 | 600 | 800 METRES | 1 |
| 0 | 200 | 400 | 600 YARDS | ½ | |

KILOMETRES
MILES

Roman fort standing out clearly below. Drop down to the road near the top of the notorious Hardknott Pass, possibly the steepest and certainly one of the most hazardous passes in the country. With severe gradients, 1:3 in places, and hairpin bends, it is definitely better to be on foot than behind a wheel here. Turn left, and where the road takes one of its many hairpin bends, on this occasion to the left, keep ahead **B** along a faint path towards the fort. Because of boggy ground, it is best not to head directly towards the fort but to keep to the higher ground on the right, crossing the former parade ground, a flat area free of boulders, to enter the fort by the east gateway.

The Romans built the fort of Mediobogdum around the end of the first and the beginning of the second century AD to guard the route over the mountains which linked the forts at Ravenglass (on the coast) with Ambleside. It conforms to the plan of most Roman forts throughout the empire, being shaped like a playing-card, with gateways along each of the four walls, and the usual arrangement of buildings inside: *principia* (head-quarters building), *praetorium* (commander's house), granaries and barracks.

On a fine day, the scenery is majestic and awe-inspiring, especially looking towards the magnificent Scafell range, but on a grey day, when the clouds and mist hang low over the fells, it looks decidedly bleak and inhospitable. It is not difficult to imagine that the 500 auxiliaries who manned the fort, mainly from the sunnier climes of Dalmatia, must have regarded service here as a penance. But even in such a small fort as this, in one of the most remote outposts of the Roman empire, they at least enjoyed the luxury of a bath house, the remains of which lie just outside the walls to the south.

From the lower end (west gateway) of the fort, follow a path down to the road and turn right. By the first group of trees and just before a cattle-grid, turn left over a footbridge, at a public foot-path sign to Eskdale and Muncaster **C**. Turn right, climb two stiles in quick succession and then keep along a fairly straight path which climbs steadily along the side of the fell, with out-standing views over Eskdale.

Pass through a gate in a wall near a stream, keep ahead and shortly recross the wall through another gate, and then continue ahead. At this point, the path, which has been clear up to now, peters out and the way becomes more difficult to follow, but keep roughly parallel with a fence on the right and, after 1½ miles (2.4km) of steady uphill walking, the route flattens out, and you arrive at the edge of the Forestry Commission

plantations of Dunnerdale Forest. These plantations began in the 1930s, and at one time would have been considerably extended over much of Eskdale and the Duddon valley, but for successful public protests.

Do not go through the gate into the forest, but turn left **D** along the boundary wall and keep straight ahead, climbing steeply across rough ground (no path) towards the summit rocks ahead. It is hard going, but the views from the summit **E** are tremendous: the Dunnerdale Fells, the Scafell range, Eskdale, the Cumbrian coast and, on the horizon, the Isle of Man. To complete a superb view, the distinctive playing-card shape of the Roman fort can be seen immediately below, standing out prominently among all the surrounding stone walls.

Now comes an equally rough and steep descent down a rocky path for about ¾ mile (1.2km), partly through trees, eventually reaching a forest road. Cross over, take the track ahead towards a farm and go through a gate, keeping to the left of the farm buildings. Bear left through another gate and follow a path through Great Wood, a small deciduous wood, delightfully refreshing after so many conifers. Near the river, a short diversion a few yards to the right brings you to Birks Bridge, which, even by Lake District standards is outstandingly picturesque and most photogenic, a pack-horse bridge which seems to have grown naturally out of the river-banks rather than to have been fashioned by the hands of man. To sit on the rocks here, by the gushing, crystal-clear green waters of the Duddon, is an ideal way of relaxing at the end of a fairly demanding walk, before returning to the car park along a grassy path on the left bank of the river to the next bridge, only ¼ mile (400m) upstream. ●

The awe-inspiring surroundings of the Roman fort at Hardknott

Place Fell and Ullswater

Start	Patterdale
Distance	8½ miles (13.7km)
Approximate time	5 hours
Parking	Small car park in Patterdale. Alternatively use car parks in Glenridding and walk along the road to Patterdale
Refreshments	Pubs and cafés in Patterdale
Ordnance Survey maps	Landranger 90 (Penrith, Keswick & Ambleside), Outdoor Leisure 5 (The English Lakes – North Eastern area)

Place Fell (2154ft/657m) is the prominent fell that lies on the eastern side of Ullswater near the head of the lake, easily seen and easily accessible from both Patterdale and Glenridding. The climb to the summit is easy to follow and not too strenuous and, as might be expected, the views from it are both dramatic and extensive. From the top, the route continues along the edge of the lonely, quiet valley of Boredale, overlooked by the bare slopes of Martindale Common, before dropping to the lake at Sandwick. The final section, along a path above the shores of Ullswater, has been described as the loveliest walk in the Lake District; praise indeed!

Patterdale, lying at the head of Ullswater and the foot of the Kirkstone Pass, gets its name from St Patrick, i.e. Patrick's Dale. According to legend, the saint came here after being shipwrecked in the Duddon estuary. Nowadays it is a bustling tourist and walking centre.

Start by walking along the main road towards Glenridding and turn right at the sign to Side Farm, where there is also a public footpath sign to Howtown and Boredale. Follow the track ahead over a footbridge and on to the farm at the foot of Place Fell. Follow the path between the buildings and turn right **Ⓐ**, at a public footpath sign to Angle Tarn and Boredale Hause, along a path which goes through a gate and gently

ascends to another one. Pass through that and immediately left through yet another gate, continuing along a path which climbs steeply for about 100 yds (91m) and then bears right to join another path which climbs along the side of the fell. On the right is a striking view of Helvellyn, with Striding Edge clearly visible, as well as a glimpse of Brothers Water at the foot of the Kirkstone Pass. The higher you get, the more superb the views and eventually a steady and continuous climb of ½ mile (800m) brings you to Boredale Hause **Ⓑ**. This flat, grassy col is the meeting-place of several paths and was once part of a pack-horse trail between Boredale and Patterdale. Here there is a cairn and the

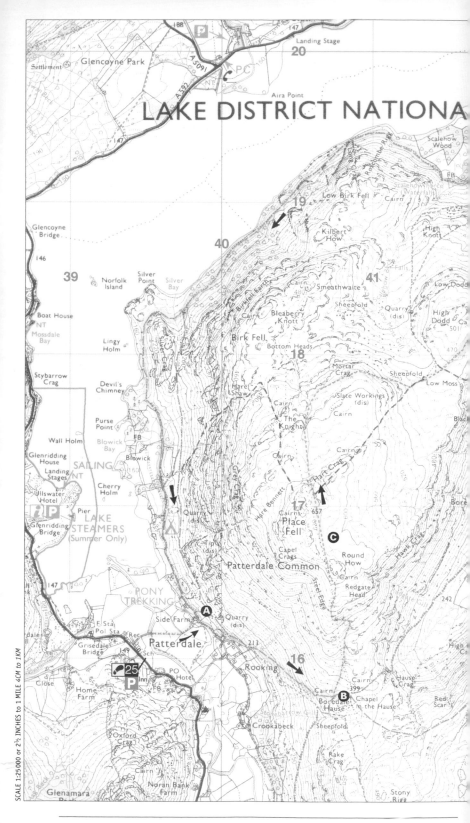

SCALE 1:25000 or 2½ INCHES to 1 MILE 4CM to 1KM

```
0    200   400   600   800 METRES  1
                                      KILOMETRES
                                      MILES
0    200   400   600 YARDS    ½
```

for a prominent cairn from which there is an even more superb view down Ullswater, and then continue, dropping down into a grassy col. At the col keep ahead, following a path over the shoulder of High Dodd, and continue high up along the edge of Boredale. After a slight descent, turn sharp right along a clear grassy path and follow it as it twists and turns downhill along the fellside. Near the bottom you join a wall on the right and keep by it through the valley, with a fine view of Hallin Fell to the right, eventually following the wall round to the right to drop steeply to a road **D**. Turn left along the road towards Sandwick but, just above the first houses, turn left again at a bridleway sign for Patterdale.

The remainder of the route is along one of the most beautiful paths in the Lake District. It follows the eastern edge of Ullswater, dipping up and down above the lake, squeezing between the fell and the lakeshore and giving the most glorious views over Ullswater, especially near the end, when, looking towards the head of the lake, you see it framed by high fells with Helvellyn peeping out above the rest. Keep along this path for nearly $3\frac{1}{2}$ miles (5.6km) to Side Farm **A**, where you turn right and retrace your steps to Patterdale. ●

fragmentary ruins of what was probably a small chapel.

At the Hause bear left along a faint grassy path which climbs gently. Soon the path becomes clearer and stretches ahead, climbing more steeply towards crags. From here there are fine views on the right over the lonely valley of Boredale, with the wild fells of Martindale and the long ridge of High Street beyond. A short but steep scramble leads to the preliminary summit of Round How and the path continues, now climbing more gently, to the final summit of Place Fell ahead **C**. From here there are glorious and extensive views of High Street, Brothers Water, Helvellyn, Gowbarrow Fell and down the length of Ullswater.

From the summit take the path ahead, making

Looking across Ullswater to Place Fell

Great Gable

Start	Seathwaite
Distance	6 miles (9.7km)
Approximate time	5 hours
Parking	Parking by roadside at Seathwaite
Refreshments	Café at Seathwaite
Ordnance Survey maps	Landrangers 89 (West Cumbria) and 90 (Penrith, Keswick & Ambleside), Outdoor Leisure 4 (The English Lakes – North Western area)

One of the best loved of Lakeland peaks, Great Gable (2949ft/899m) is surrounded by some of the wildest and most dramatic mountain terrain in the country. There are several possible starting points for an ascent, but the one from Seathwaite offers both variety and scenic splendour. A lengthy climb by the side of Sourmilk Gill continues through Gillercomb and on to the 2603ft (801m) high summit of Green Gable, the launching pad for the final climb to the top of Great Gable itself. A steep descent to Styhead Tarn is followed by an easy walk down Styhead Pass, using either the popular route via Stockley Bridge or a route via Taylorgill Force. This is a walk for a fine day, and you need to be reasonably fit to tackle it.

From the roadside parking-area make your way up to Seathwaite, which lies at the head of Borrowdale and has the dubious distinction of being the wettest place in England, with an average annual rainfall of around 125in (3180mm).

Turn right through a gate in the farm buildings, at a public footpath sign, and take the path ahead over the infant River Derwent and up the left-hand side of Sourmilk Gill. The well-surfaced path zigzags steeply up the side of a waterfall, giving lovely views to the right down Borrowdale and involving some scrambling here and there. On the other side of the gill, spoil-heaps mark the entrance of an abandoned graphite mine; the mining of graphite flourished in this area in the 16th and 17th

centuries, and was the foundation of the Keswick pencil industry. Pass through a gate, continue up to the top of the fall and bear left **A** to pick up a path that keeps along the left-hand side of Gillercomb, between the crags of Grey Knotts on the right and Base Brown on the left. It is a long, and towards the end, steep climb to the head of the valley. Here you turn right and keep ahead along a path lined with cairns to the summit of Green Gable **B**. The superb view of Scafell Pike, Buttermere,

Fleetwith Pike and Ennerdale is but an appetiser of what is to come.

Continue ahead, dropping down into a col called Windy Gap, followed by the final assault on Great Gable, scrambling towards the summit along a cairned route. For the final 200 yds (183m), the path flattens out somewhat and heads across the rocks to the summit cairn **C**. Here there is a bronze memorial, fixed to one of the summit stones, to twenty-four members of the Fell and Rock Climbing Club of the English Lake District (founded in 1907). Each year a short service is held here on Remembrance Sunday. Nearly 1200 acres (485 ha) of the surrounding area were bought in 1923 and presented to the National Trust in memory of the members of the club who died in the First World War. The view from the top over Buttermere, Ennerdale, Scafell Pike and Langdale is outstanding; well worth the effort, especially from the Westmorland Cairn, about 100 yds (91m) further on from the summit, where there is a magnificent vista down Wasdale to Wast Water.

From the summit, take the cairned path to the south (easily seen), which drops down steeply towards Styhead Tarn. Ahead is a fine view of the path that leads up via Sprinkling Tarn to the summit of Scafell Pike. At the bottom, turn left to join a broad path **D**, the Styhead Pass, once a pack-horse trail between Borrowdale and Wasdale. Proposals have been made to construct a road over the Styhead Pass but mercifully they have never been followed up. Pass the tarn and along to a footbridge **E**.

There is a choice of routes back to Seathwaite: either cross the bridge and follow the right-hand side of the beck to Stockley Bridge or keep ahead along the left-hand side through the wooded ravine and waterfalls of Taylorgill. The first is the more straightforward and popular, the second is more difficult though more spectacular, and this path is not so well defined; either way there are glorious views all the while looking down Borrowdale.

SCALE 1:27777 or about 2¼ INCHES to 1 MILE 3.6CM to 1KM

Helvellyn

Start	Glenridding
Distance	8½ miles (13.7km)
Approximate time	6 hours
Parking	Glenridding
Refreshments	Pubs and cafés in Glenridding
Ordnance Survey maps	Landranger 90 (Penrith, Keswick & Ambleside), Outdoor Leisure 5 (The English Lakes – North Eastern area)

England's third-highest mountain and one of Lakeland's most frequently climbed summits, Helvellyn offers a challenging and exciting fell walk and rewards the fit and energetic walker with a variety of terrain, dramatic scenery and distant views. After a lengthy, tiring climb along the edge of Grisedale, the final route to the summit is along the spectacular long ridge of Striding Edge, followed by a rough scramble. The descent begins along the companion ridge of Swirral Edge before levelling off and dropping down. Although the edges are not as difficult as they appear from a distance, great care must be exercised on the traverse of both of them. Unless you are an experienced fellwalker able to use a compass, this walk should definitely not be attempted in poor weather.

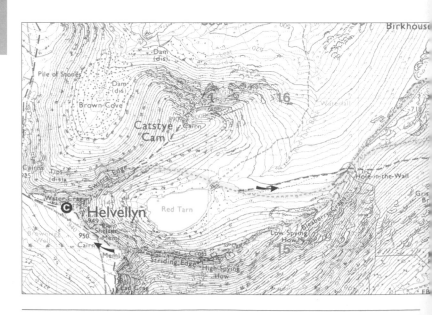

Glenridding, once a lead-mining village, lies near the head of Ullswater, England's second-longest lake, surrounded by high fells. As well as being a good centre for walking, a number of popular and scenic boat trips operate from the pier.

Start by walking along the main road towards Patterdale – a permissive path runs parallel to the road for much of the way. Just past the Patterdale sign, cross Grisedale Bridge and turn right **Ⓐ** along a lane that bears right, following the beck in its wooded valley below. At a public footpath sign, turn right along a rough track **Ⓑ**, cross the beck and keep ahead to a gate. Go through, continue to another gate, go through that and turn left along a path that

climbs steadily along the side of Grisedale, with excellent views towards the head of the dale framed by the peaks of St Sunday Crag and Dollywagon Pike.

A long, relentless climb of 1500ft (457m) over 1$\frac{1}{2}$ miles (2.4km) brings you to a stile in a wall known affectionately to walkers as the Hole-in-the-Wall. Climb over and keep ahead, following a line of cairns through a wilderness of rocks to a large pile of boulders called High Spying How. Negotiate these, keeping along the right-hand edge, and the 300-yd (276m) long Striding Edge is ahead. From a distance, or from photographs, Striding Edge looks positively hair-raising, giving the impression that you have to walk along a razor's edge of rocks. Although it is an exciting ridge walk, which must be treated with respect,

| 0 | 200 | 400 | 600 | 800 METRES | 1 |
| 0 | 200 | 400 | 600 YARDS | ½ | |

KILOMETRES
MILES

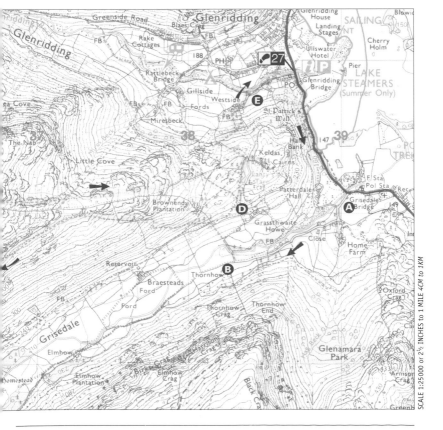

SCALE 1:25 000 or 2½ INCHES to 1 MILE 4CM to 1KM

it is not as dangerous as it looks, except in high winds, when it is definitely to be avoided. You are on it almost before you realise and there is a path a few yards below the ridge to the right. It is a tremendously exhilarating feeling to walk along it, with the crags on the right plunging down steeply to Red Tarn and the summit crest of Helvellyn just ahead. The most difficult section is scrambling over another awkward tower of rocks at the end. Now comes the final haul to the summit (3118ft/ 949m) – some more steep, rough scrambling that brings you to the Gough memorial stone. This marks the spot where the body of Charles Gough was discovered in 1803. He had been killed by a rock fall and when his skeletal remains were found three months later his dog was still guarding the body. After this sobering experience, it is but a short distance across the flat plateau to the summit wall **C** from where in clear conditions there are incredible views over a large proportion of the Lake District, including Coniston Old Man, the Langdale Pikes, the Scafell range, Great Gable, High Street, Harter Fell, Gowbarrow Fell, the Derwent Fells, Blencathra and Skiddaw. Just to the south of the summit wall, a stone commemorates the alleged first landing of an aeroplane on a British mountain, in 1926.

Keep ahead along the summit edge and by a cairn turn sharp right to descend along Swirral Edge, which is similar to, though less awe-inspiring than, Striding Edge. Descend steeply with a fine view of Catstye Cam ahead, and after a while the path bears right, off the ridge, and drops down to the corner of Red Tarn. At this point there is a clear view of much of your recent route: Red Tarn lying in a natural amphitheatre with Striding Edge and Swirral Edge forming the two sides of it and pointing the way, like thin fingers, to the summit of Helvellyn. Cross a beck near the outlet from the tarn, bear slightly left and head across rough open country towards the line of crags on the right. There is no obvious path at this stage, but if you keep roughly parallel with, and just below, the line of crags, you pick up a path and after just over $\frac{1}{2}$ mile (800m) arrive at a ladder-stile about 100 yds (91m) below the Hole-in-the-Wall.

Do not climb the stile but turn left along a path that keeps by the wall on the right, heading downhill with views over Ullswater all the while. Near an outstanding viewpoint over Glenridding and Ullswater the path bears left away from the wall and heads down to a valley, but at this point keep straight ahead over the small hill in front and drop down to a ladder-stile by a wall corner. Climb over, turn right through a gate a few yards ahead, then turn left and continue down to the tree-encircled Lanty's Tarn, a lovely, quiet, half-hidden spot **D**. Turn left at the tarn, go through a gate and make a brief detour to the right for one more minor ascent – to the top of Keldas. This is little more than a knoll but from it there is a fine view down Ullswater – possibly the finest view of all, with the waters of the lake framed by pine trees. This is an ideal spot to relax before the final, short drop into Glenridding.

Return to the gate by the tarn and keep ahead along a broad, stony path that heads downhill. On reaching a gate, do not go through it but turn sharp right down to another gate; go through this gate and turn left through woodland to yet another gate. Go through that, turn right along a track **E** and keep by the side of Glenridding Beck on the left, back to the starting point. ●

Coniston Old Man and Coniston Water

Start	Coniston
Distance	9 miles (14.5km)
Approximate time	5½ hours
Parking	Coniston
Refreshments	Pubs and cafés in Coniston, pubs in Torver
Ordnance Survey maps	Landranger 96 (Barrow-in-Furness and South Lakeland), Outdoor Leisure 6 (The English Lakes – South Western area)

The conical peak of the Old Man (2635ft/803m) dominates the village of Coniston. This walk combines a mountain climb and a lakeside stroll. The ascent of the Old Man is lengthy and, towards the end, steep, but it is not difficult and is followed by a gradual descent to Torver and a relaxing walk through woods and across meadows adjoining the western shores of Coniston Water.

Coniston is an excellent walking centre, and an added attraction is that from here you may take a trip around the lake in the National Trust's Victorian steam gondola. One of the stopping places is Brantwood, home of John Ruskin (who is buried in Coniston churchyard), which is seen near the end of the walk. Coniston Water is also associated with the attempts by Sir Malcolm and Donald Campbell to break the world water-speed record, culminating in Donald Campbell's death in 1967 when trying to reach a speed of 300 miles (483km) per hour.

From the car park turn left along the road, past the church, over the bridge and turn right along a narrow lane to the Sun Hotel. Turn right along the side of the hotel **Ⓐ**, at a public footpath sign to Old Man and Levers Water, go through a gate by a farm and keep ahead along a broad track that heads gently up a wooded valley towards the fells in front,

keeping by the tumbling waters of Levers Water Beck. This is the popular route to the Old Man, but it is some-times criticised for being less attractive than the others because it passes by the ruined huts and spoil tips of slate quarries and copper mines; these do add interest, however, as the mountain has a long industrial history and has been continuously exploited for its mineral resources and beautiful green slate.

Climb a ladder-stile to get a most impressive view of Coniston Old Man ahead, and keep along a path that curves around, ascending all the while. Continue past old quarries and ruined buildings, climbing more steeply up a winding path, conveniently marked by cairns, to the small tarn of Low Water. Now comes the final steep climb through crags and boulders to the summit **Ⓑ**, from where there is a glorious view over Coniston Water, Windermere, Morecambe Bay, the Furness Peninsula, the Langdale

Pikes, Dunnerdale Fells and, beyond, the Scafell range.

Keep straight ahead past the summit along a ridge and, after about 200 yds (183m), bear slightly left off the ridge and keep following the path around to the left and downhill towards the base of the steep slopes of Dow Crag. At 2555ft (778m) Dow Crag is only marginally lower than Coniston Old Man, and its forbidding cliffs, which plunge almost sheer down to Goat's Water, are a favourite haunt of rock-climbers. Descend to a col and turn left along a path that drops steeply to follow the left-hand edge of Goat's Water. Past this delightful tarn, keep ahead along the side of a valley, with a stream on the right and fine views ahead all the while over Coniston Water, and beyond to Morecambe Bay and the line of the Pennines. About ³⁄₄ mile (1.2km) after leaving the tarn, you reach a broad track, the Walna Scar Road. Cross it and keep ahead, making towards the banks of the stream. After passing a waterfall on the right, continue through a slate quarry, rejoining the stream and heading down to cross a footbridge. Go through a gate, keep ahead a few yards to another gate, turn left through it, ahead to yet another gate, through that and take the path ahead between a wire fence and a wall. Pass through another gate and continue along a walled track to Torver, bearing sharp left past houses and down a tarmac drive to a road **C**.

The village is to the right; the route continues by turning left over the bridge and immediately right through a kissing-gate, at a public footpath sign to the lake. Walk along the edge of a field, passing a house on the left and, at the end of a fence on the left, keep ahead across the field to a stile. Climb over, continue to another stile a few yards in front, climb that, go through a gap in the wall ahead, and proceed

uphill to a gate and stile. Go through, cross a lane and continue along a broad path. Over to the left is a fine view of the Old Man. Keep along this well-sign-posted path down through the attractive woodland of Torver Common Wood to the shores of Coniston Water **D**.

Turn left along the lakeside path and keep along it for 1¹⁄₄ miles (2km), through woods and across meadows, through gates and over stiles, with superb views all the while across the lake. The prominent house on the other side is Brantwood, home of John Ruskin between 1871 and 1900. He loved the Lake District and especially this house with its beautiful views over the lake to the mountains beyond.

Areas of clinker by the lakeshore are an indication that small-scale iron-

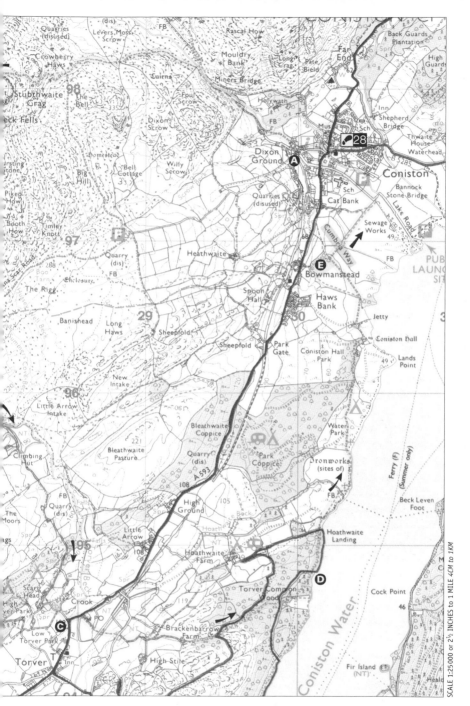

SCALE 1:25 000 or 2½ INCHES to 1 MILE 4CM to 1KM

smelting once took place here. The path passes by Coniston Hall, a fine 15th-century manor-house with circular chimney-stacks. Just beyond the hall, the path bears left away from the lake, heading towards the village. Bear right

E, go through a gate and turn left, following a wire fence on the left, along the edge of a field. At the end of that field, turn left over a stile and along the road ahead into Coniston. Turn right at the main road to the village centre. ●

Further Information

The National Parks and Countryside Recreation

Ten National Parks were created in England and Wales as a result of an Act of Parliament in 1949. In addition to these, there are numerous specially designated Areas of Outstanding Natural Beauty, Country and Regional Parks, Sites of Special Scientific Interest and picnic areas scattered throughout England, Wales and Scotland, all of which share the twin aims of preservation of the countryside and public accessibility and enjoyment.

John Dower, whose report in 1945 created their framework, defined a National Park as 'an extensive area of beautiful and relatively wild country in which, for the nation's benefit and by appropriate national decision and action, (a) the characteristic landscape beauty is strictly preserved, (b) access and facilities for public open-air enjoyment are amply provided, (c) wildlife and buildings and places of architectural and historic interest are suitably protected, while (d) established farming use is effectively maintained'.

Proposals for the creation of areas of protected countryside were first made before World War I, but nothing was done. The growing demand for access to open country and the reluctance of landowners – particularly those who owned large expanses of uncultivated moorland – to grant it led to a number of ugly incidents, in particular the mass trespass in the Peak District in 1932, when ramblers and gamekeepers came to blows and some trespassers received stiff prison sentences.

It was after World War II that calls for countryside conservation and access came to fruition in parliament. The National Parks and Countryside Act of 1949 provided for the designation and preservation of areas both of great scenic beauty and of particular wildlife and scientific interest throughout Britain. More specifically it provided for the

Stockley Bridge – on the return path from Great Gable to Seathwaite

creation of National Parks in England and Wales. Scotland was excluded because, with greater areas of open space and a smaller population, there were fewer pressures on the Scottish countryside.

A National Parks Commission, a forerunner of the Countryside Commission, was set up, and over the next eight years ten areas were designated as parks; seven in England (Northumberland, Lake District, North York Moors, Yorkshire Dales, Peak District, Exmoor and Dartmoor) and three in Wales (Snowdonia, Brecon Beacons and Pembrokeshire Coast). In 1989 the Norfolk and Suffolk Broads were added to the list. At the same time the Commission was also given the responsibility for designating other smaller areas of high recreational and scenic qualities (Areas of Outstanding Natural Beauty), plus the power to propose and develop long-distance footpaths, now called National Trails.

The authorities who administer the individual National Parks have the very difficult task of reconciling the interests of the people who live and earn their living within them with those of visitors. National Parks are not living museums and there is pressure to exploit the resources of the area, through more intensive farming, or through increased quarrying and forestry, extraction of minerals or the construction of reservoirs.

In the end it all comes down to a question of balance – between conservation and 'sensitive development'. On the one hand there is a responsibility to preserve the natural beauty of the National Parks and to promote their enjoyment by the public, and on the other, the needs and well-being of the people living and working in them have to be borne in mind.

The National Trust

Anyone who likes visiting places of natural beauty and/or historic interest has cause to be grateful to the National Trust. Without it, many such places would probably have vanished by now.

It was in response to the pressures on the countryside posed by the relentless march of Victorian industrialisation that the trust was set up in 1895. Its founders, inspired by the common goals of protecting and conserving Britain's national heritage and widening public access to it, were Sir Robert Hunter, Octavia Hill and Canon Rawnsley: respectively a solicitor, a social reformer and a clergyman. The latter was particularly influential. As a canon of Carlisle Cathedral and vicar of Crosthwaite (near Keswick), he was concerned about threats to the Lake District and had already been active in protecting footpaths and promoting public access to open countryside. After the flooding of Thirlmere in 1879 to create a large reservoir, he became increasingly convinced that the only effective way to guarantee protection was outright ownership of land.

The purpose of the National Trust is to preserve areas of natural beauty and sites of historic interest by acquisition, holding them in trust for the nation and making them available for public access and enjoyment. Some of its properties have been acquired through purchase, but many have been donated. Nowadays it is not only one of the biggest landowners in

the country, but also one of the most active conservation charities, protecting 581,113 acres (253,176 ha) of land, including 555 miles (892km) of coastline, and over 300 historic properties in England, Wales and Northern Ireland. (There is a separate National Trust for Scotland, which was set up in 1931.)

Furthermore, once a piece of land has come under National Trust ownership, it is difficult for its status to be altered. As a result of parliamentary legislation in 1907, the Trust was given the right to declare its property inalienable, so ensuring that in any subsequent dispute it can appeal directly to parliament.

As it works towards its dual aims of conserving areas of attractive countryside and encouraging greater public access (not easy to reconcile in this age of mass tourism), the Trust provides an excellent service for walkers by creating new concessionary paths and waymarked trails, maintaining stiles and footbridges and combating the ever-increasing problem of footpath erosion.

For details of membership, contact the National Trust at the address on page 95.

The Ramblers' Association

No organisation works more actively to protect and extend the rights and interests of walkers in the countryside than the Ramblers' Association. Its aims are clear: to foster a greater knowledge, love and care of the countryside; to assist in the protection and enhancement of public rights of way and areas of natural beauty; to work for greater public access to the countryside; and to encourage more people to take up rambling as a healthy, recreational leisure activity.

It was founded in 1935 when, following the setting up of a National Council of Ramblers' Federations in 1931, a number of federations earlier formed in London, Manchester, the Midlands and elsewhere came together to create a more effective pressure group, to deal with such problems as the disappearance and obstruction of footpaths, the prevention of access to open mountain and moorland and increasing hostility from landowners. This was the era of the mass trespasses, when there were sometimes violent confrontations between ramblers and gamekeepers, especially on the moorlands of the Peak District.

Since then the Ramblers' Association has played an influential role in preserving and developing the national footpath network, supporting the creation of national parks and encouraging the designation and way-marking of long-distance routes.

Our freedom to walk in the countryside is precarious and requires constant vigilance. As well as the perennial problems of footpaths being illegally obstructed, disappearing through lack of use or extinguished by housing or road construction, new dangers can spring up at any time.

It is to meet such problems and dangers that the Ramblers' Association exists and represents the interests of all walkers. The address to write to for information on the Ramblers' Association and how to become a member is given on page 95.

Walkers and the Law

The average walker in a national park or other popular walking area, armed with the appropriate Ordnance Survey map, reinforced perhaps by a guidebook giving detailed walking instructions, is unlikely to run into legal difficulties, but it is useful to know something about the law relating to public rights of way. The right to walk over certain parts of the countryside has developed over a long period, and how such rights came into being is a complex subject, too lengthy to be discussed here. The following comments are intended simply as a helpful guide, backed up by the Countryside Access Charter, a concise summary of walkers' rights and obligations drawn up by the Countryside Commission.

Basically there are two main kinds of public rights of way: footpaths (for walkers only) and bridleways (for walkers, riders on horseback and pedal cyclists).

Footpaths and bridleways are shown by broken green lines on Ordnance Survey Pathfinder and Outdoor Leisure maps and broken red lines on Landranger maps. There is also a third category, called byways: chiefly broad tracks (green lanes) or farm roads, which walkers, riders and cyclists have to share, usually only occasionally, with motor vehicles. Many of these public paths have been in existence for hundreds of years and some even originated as prehistoric trackways and have been in constant use for well over 2000 years. Ways known as RUPPs (roads used as public paths) still appear on some maps. The legal definition of such byways is ambiguous and they are gradually being reclassified as footpaths, bridleways or byways.

The term 'right of way' means exactly what it says. It gives right of passage over what, in the vast majority of cases, is private land, and you are required to keep to the line of the path and not stray on to the land on either side. If you inadvertently wander off the right of way – either because of faulty map-reading or because the route is not clearly indicated on the ground – you are technically trespassing and the wisest course is to ask the nearest available person (farmer or fellow walker) to direct you back to the correct route. There are stories about unpleasant confrontations between walkers and farmers at times, but in general most farmers are co-operative when responding to a genuine and polite request for assistance in route-finding.

Obstructions can sometimes be a problem and probably the most common of these is where a path across a field has been ploughed up. It is legal for a farmer to plough up a path provided that he restores it within two weeks, barring exceptionally bad weather. This does not always happen and here the walker is presented with a dilemma: to follow the line of the path, even if this inevitably means treading on crops, or to walk around the edge of the field. The latter course of action often seems the best but this means that you would be trespassing

Countryside Access Charter

Your rights of way are:

- public footpaths – on foot only. Sometimes waymarked in yellow
- bridleways – on foot, horseback and pedal cycle. Sometimes waymarked in blue
- byways (usually old roads), most 'roads used as public paths' and, of course, public roads – all traffic has the right of way

Use maps, signs and waymarks to check rights of way. Ordnance Survey Pathfinder and Landranger maps show most public rights of way

On rights of way you can:

- take a pram, pushchair or wheelchair if practicable
- take a dog (on a lead or under close control)
- take a short route round an illegal obstruction or remove it sufficiently to get past

You have a right to go for recreation to:

- public parks and open spaces – on foot
- most commons near older towns and cities – on foot and sometimes on horseback
- private land where the owner has a formal agreement with the local authority

In addition you can use the following by local or established custom or consent, but ask for advice if you are unsure:

- many areas of open country, such as moorland, fell and coastal areas, especially those in the care of the National Trust, and some commons
- some woods and forests, especially those owned by the Forestry Commission
- country parks and picnic sites
- most beaches
- canal towpaths
- some private paths and tracks Consent sometimes extends to horse-riding and cycling

For your information:

- county councils and London boroughs maintain and record rights of way, and register commons
- obstructions, dangerous animals, harassment and misleading signs on rights of way are illegal and you should report them to the county council
- paths across fields can be ploughed, but must normally be reinstated within two weeks
- landowners can require you to leave land to which you have no right of access
- motor vehicles are normally permitted only on roads, byways and some 'roads used as public paths'

and not keeping to the exact line of the path. In the case of other obstructions which may block a path (illegal fences and locked gates etc), common sense has to be used in order to negotiate them by the easiest method – detour or removal. You should only ever remove as much as is necessary to get through, and if you can easily go round the obstruction without causing any damage, then you should do so. If you have any problems negotiating rights of way, you should report the matter to the rights of way department of the relevant council, which will take action with the landowner concerned.

Apart from rights of way enshrined by law, there are a number of other paths available to walkers. Permissive or

concessionary paths have been created where a landowner has given permission for the public to use a particular route across his land. The main problem with these is that, as they have been granted as a concession, there is no legal right to use them and therefore they can be extinguished at any time. In practice, many of these concessionary routes have been established on land owned either by large public bodies such as the Forestry Commission, or by a private one, such as the National Trust, and as these mainly encourage walkers to use their paths, they are unlikely to be closed unless a change of ownership occurs.

Walkers also have free access to country parks (except where requested to keep away from certain areas for ecological reasons, e.g. wildlife protection, woodland regeneration, safeguarding of rare plants etc), canal towpaths and most beaches. By custom, though not by right, you are generally free to walk across the open and uncultivated higher land of mountain, moorland and fell, but this varies from area to area and from one season to another – grouse moors, for example, will be out of bounds during the breeding and shooting seasons and some open areas are used as Ministry of Defence firing ranges, for which reason access will be restricted. In some areas the situation has been clarified as a result of 'access agreements' between the landowners and either the county council or the national park authority, which clearly define when and where you can walk over such open country.

Ullswater from Keldas, just above Glenridding

 ### Safety on the Hills

The hills, mountains and moorlands of Britain, though of modest height compared with those in many other countries, need to be treated with respect. Friendly and inviting in good weather, they can quickly be transformed into wet, misty, windswept and potentially dangerous areas of wilderness in bad weather. Even on an outwardly fine and settled summer day, conditions can rapidly deteriorate at high altitudes and, in winter, even more so.

Therefore it is advisable to always take both warm and waterproof clothing, sufficient nourishing food, a hot drink, first-aid kit, torch and whistle. Wear suitable footwear, such as strong walking-boots or shoes that give a good grip over rocky terrain and on slippery slopes. Try to obtain a local weather forecast and bear it in mind before you start. Do not be afraid to abandon your proposed route

and return to your starting point in the event of a sudden and unexpected deterioration in the weather. Do not go alone and allow enough time to finish the walk well before nightfall.

Most of the walks described in this book do not venture into remote wilderness areas and will be safe to do, given due care and respect, at any time of year in all but the most unreasonable weather. Indeed, a crisp, fine winter day often provides perfect walking conditions, with firm ground underfoot and a clarity that is not possible to achieve in the other seasons of the year. A few walks, however, are suitable only for reasonably fit and experienced hill walkers able to use a compass and should definitely not be tackled by anyone else during the winter months or in bad weather, especially high winds and mist. These are indicated in the general description that precedes each of the walks.

Useful Organisations

Council for National Parks
246 Lavender Hill, London SW11 1LJ.
Tel. 020 7924 4077

Council for the Protection of Rural England
25 Buckingham Palace Road,
London SW1W 0PP. Tel. 020 7976 6433

Countryside Agency
John Dower House, Crescent Place,
Cheltenham, Gloucestershire GL50 3RA.
Tel. 01242 521381

Cumbria Tourist Board
Ashleigh, Holly Road,
Windermere, Cumbria LA23 2AQ.
Tel. 015394 44444

Forestry Commission
Information Dept, 231 Corstorphine Road,
Edinburgh EH12 7AT. Tel. 0131 334 0303

Friends of the Lake District
Murley Moss, Oxenholme Road, Kendal,
Cumbria LA9 7SS. Tel. 01539 720788

Lake District National Park Authority
information centres *(*not open all year)*:
*Ambleside: 01539 432729
*Bowness Bay: 015394 42895
*Broughton-in-Furness: 01229 716115
*Coniston: 015394 41533
*Glenridding: 017684 82414
*Grasmere: 015394 35245
*Hawkshead: 015394 36525
Keswick: 017687 72645
*Pooley Bridge: 017684 86530
*Seatoller: 017687 77294
*Waterhead: 015394 32729

Lake District National Park Visitor Centre
Brockhole, Windermere, Cumbria LA23 1LJ.
Tel. 015394 46601

Long Distance Walkers' Association
21 Upcroft, Windsor, Berkshire SL4 3NH.
Tel. 01753 866685

National Trust
Membership and general enquiries:
PO Box 39, Bromley, Kent BR1 3XL.
Tel. 020 8315 1111
North-west regional office:
The Hollens, Grasmere, Ambleside,
Cumbria LA22 9QZ. Tel. 015394 35599

Ordnance Survey
Romsey Road, Maybush,
Southampton SO16 4GU.
Tel. 08456 05 05 05 (Lo-call)

Ramblers' Association
2nd Floor, Camelford House, 87–90 Albert
Embankment, London SE1 7TW.
Tel. 020 7339 8500

Ravenglass and Eskdale Railway
Ravenglass, Cumbria CA18 1SW.
Tel. 01229 717278

Youth Hostels Association
Trevelyan House, 8 St Stephen's Hill,
St Albans, Hertfordshire AL1 2DY.
Tel. 01727 855215.

 ## Ordnance Survey Maps of the Lake District

The Lake District is covered by Ordnance Survey 1:50 000 (1¼ inches to 1 mile or 2cm to 1km) scale Landranger map sheets 89, 90, 96 and 97). These all-purpose maps are packed with information to help you explore the area. Viewpoints, picnic sites, places of interest and caravan and camping sites are shown, as well as public rights of way information such as footpaths and bridleways.

To examine the Lake District in more detail, and especially if you are planning walks, Ordnance Survey Outdoor Leisure maps at 1:25 000 (2½ inches to 1 mile or 4cm to 1km) scale are ideal. Four such maps cover the main Lake District National Park:

Sheet 4 – The English Lakes –
 North Western area
Sheet 5 – The English Lakes –
 North Eastern area
Sheet 6 – The English Lakes –
 South Western area
Sheet 7 – The English Lakes –
 South Eastern area

The Lake District area is also covered by Ordnance Survey Touring map number 3, at 1 inch to 1 mile (approx. 2.5cm to 1.6km) scale, which includes useful guide information on the reverse.

To get to the Lake District, use the Ordnance Survey Great Britain Route-planner Travelmaster map number 1 at 1:625 000 (1 inch to 10 miles or 1cm to 6.25km) scale or Travelmaster map 5 (Northern England) at 1:250 000 (1 inch to 4 miles or 1cm to 2.5km) scale.

Ordnance Survey maps and guides are available from most booksellers, stationers and newsagents.

Index

Entries in *italic type* refer to illustrations